The

Beginning Of Kabbalah Wisdoms

rules & statements 226

An Introduction to Kabbalistic thought

The Kabbalist Rabbi

Kolomous Kalman Altessler

Simchatchaim.com

There is no known book without mistakes. Therefore, I ask in every language of application if anyone has any questions, comments, clarifications, corrections, please send to: **book@simchatchaim.com**

All material used in this section may not be used for commercial purposes, but only for study and teaching.

To get this book or books and information Email me at: **book@simchatchaim.com**

Copyright©All Rights Reserved to

www.simchatchaim.com

YBS©All rights reserved to the author

First Edition 2023

TABLE OF CONTENTS

Page	Contents
3	Introduction
5	Chapter One
19	Chapter Two
29	Chapter Three
45	Chapter Four
49	Chapter Five
57	Chapter Six
73	Chapter Seven
81	Chapter Eight
97	Chapter Nine
113	Chapter Ten

Please note that there are few paragraphs that could not be translated. The reference sources are not translated as they are in Hebrew. Theses are all referred to in the Hebrew sections of the book.

Pamphlet
Rules of the beginning of the wisdom of Kabbalah
Rules for beginners to learn the knowledge of the beginning of the wisdom of Kabbalah
The wisdom of truth
It is an important book that teaches the internal part of the Torah.
Founded according to the commentaries of the Gr'a and R'amchal Luzzatto in the Ar"i z"l writings.
The Zohar HaKadosh, the other Kabbalistic books from the letters of the late Ariz"l:
Rules and monikers read in the names of the Sefirot found in the Holy Zohar and the writings of the late Ari, as well as the monikers and names found in the commentary on the sacred tree of the late Maharshal (printed in the city of Shklav, in the year 1845) All this was composed by one special rabbi, a famous genius and tzaddik, Ar"i.
It is copied from his own holy manuscripts, and arranged by Rabbi Aharon Meir ben Rabbi Altshuler.
Rabbi Aharon Meir ben Rabbi Altshuler is from the holy city of Mariupal. He is the grandson and great grandson of the genius and righteous Kabbalist Rabbi Klonimus Kalman Z"L.
This book was printed in Hebrew in the city of Warsaw
In the printing press of the Schuldberb brothers, Dzika 1 No. Year 1853

The Beginning of Kabbalah Wisdom - Introduction

Introduction

Tells his words to Yaakov...... (Psalms147 19)

The contents of this book, is precious. For it is an introduction and introduction of the rules to the peace of the faithful of the children of Israel in their hearts, who longed to come inside the gates marked by the wisdom of truth, and to learn and understand the words of honesty and words of truth, the writings of the late Ar"i Z"L.

However, as they have lost knowledge of these ways of learning wisdom, they explore blindly around the gates of wisdom. Their hearts do not open for them to the understanding of the eternal wisdom of the Torah. Their understanding is limited early. They lack the introductions and rules needed for this wisdom.

This book will enlighten their eyes with the help of the blessed name. Although it is small in quantity, it is high in quality. For in it they will find every object of their heart. For he teaches the knowledge of wisdom, and the rules of truth of the Torat Emet (Wisdom of Kabbalah). The wisdom is precious and priceless.

The book also guides you on the path of truth and the straight path in reason and knowledge - the order of study in the books of the Kabbalists and the manner of their study. How to ascend higher and higher, until the light reaches the halls of NOGA, the supreme wisdom and radiance of Kabbalah, in a very sublime way. And all its introductions and rules, are founded on the foundations of truth and the greatest Kabbalistic Rabbis of the world. The non-existent books of the late Rabbi Moshe Chaim Luzzatto, and according to the commentaries and explanations of the late Gr'a in the Holy Zohar and the writings of the late Ar"i and a book of creation (Sefer Yetzirah). According to the rules and introductions of the Tree of Life and the Fruit of the Tree of Life, and the other writings of the late Ar"i.

And for the sages who are already inside the halls of wisdom, I hope that this book will be pleasing to them, because they will have clarity in their eyes, by which they will hold in their hearts a knowledge of wisdom which is scattered among several books, and hidden in various places. Here in this book there is 226 rules and statements that are bundled together.

And in this I will come to the conclusion of standing at the gate to speak. For if there is more to mention - the article of the sage

The Beginning of Kabbalah Wisdom - Introduction

Shlomo HaMelech. The beginning of wisdom is the fear of the LORD Know faithfully. This is the main thing for the whole house of Israel, and especially for every individual. Those who love me I love, and those who seek me will find me (Mishle 8:17). Then the above-mentioned Shlomo HaMelech will be fulfilled in them - For he who finds me, finds life and obtains favor from the God. am a lover of God, for I have found life in God, as the good will of their souls, Amen:

Chapter 1

1. Since G-d is not confined to time and space or any other limitations, Kabbalah refers to Him as **Ayn Sof** - The Infinite. As He is infinite and boundless, so is the power of His Will.

2. The prohibition against the contemplation of G-d's essence is widely known. Whatever is related about G-d pertains only to His Will and providence, which are manifest by His actions. This general rule applies to all Kabbalah, as stated by Rabbeinu Moshe Chaim Luzzatto in his book Adir Bamarom, "It is self evident that any expression regarding the Emanator, Blessed Be He, refers only to His actions rather than His essence."

3. There are ten Sefirot by which G-d, Blessed Be He, creates and conducts the worlds. They Are:

    A. Keter - Crown,
    B. Chochmah - Wisdom,
    C. Binah - Understanding,
    D. Chessed - Kindness,

E. Gevurah - Might,
F. Tiferet - Beauty,
G. Netzac - Victory,
H. Hod - Majesty,
I. Yesod - Foundation,
J. Malchut - Kingdom.

<pre>
                Keter
    Binah   Chochmah
                Tiferet
    Gevurah   Chessed
                Yesod
    Hod   Netzach
               Malchut
</pre>

4. The Sefirot are those divine faculties which G-d utilizes to create and conduct the worlds.

5. G-d governs the world with three general modes of conduct; Pure Kindness - Chessed, Pure Judgment - Din, and the median conduct of Mercy - Rachamim.

6. Keter influences great and unbounded kindness and mercy without discerning the merit of the recipient. This is because Keter represents G-d's ultimate intention in creation, that is to benefit All, as the Talmud states on the verse, "I will be gracious to whomever I will be gracious," - even to the unworthy.

7. Chochmah, too, is free of Judgement, influencing the world with great kindness including the unworthy, but, not to the extent of Keter. The quality of Binah is kindness as well, yet to a lesser degree. This is because judgments begin to arise in Binah, as mentioned in the blessing: "Who gives the rooster the understanding (Binah) to discern (Judgment) between day and night," - For sometimes, in order to prevent anarchy, G-d excercises judgment upon the world, so that evil, though a necessary component in creation for the purpose of choise, not be left unchecked. This judgment, in truth, is a kindness to the world. Moreover, kindness may be the motivating factor of severity, as scripture states, "For whom the L-rd loves, He corrects," and, "As a man chastens his son so does the L-rd your G-d chasten you."

8. Keter, Chochmah, and Binah are called the first or upper three sefirot. When any of these are revealed, it is a time of great mercy and goodwill toward the world. They reflect G-d's ultimate intention in the world, unobstructed by the deeds of man.

9. Chesed is Pure Kindness, though only to the meritorious, as is the reward of the righteous in Gan Eden. Gevurah is Pure Judgment and retribution to the guilty, as is the punishment of the wicked in Genhenom. Tiferet is the median conduct of Mercy, between Chesed and Gevurah, but inclines more toward Kindness than Judgment.

10. Netzach is Kindness tempered with Judgment, for example, sometimes the righteous suffer in this world for their few errors, to be ultimately rewarded in the world to come - the seemingly negative being ultimately positive.

11. Hod is Judgment tempered with Kindness, for example, sometimes the wicked prosper in this world for their few virtues, to be ultimately destroyed in the world to come, as scripture states, "He pays his enemy up front to destroy him," - the seemingly positive being ultimately negative. Yesod is the median conduct between Netzach and Hod, tempered by both, but inclining more toward Judgment than Kindness. The world is generally conducted through this faculty.

12. The six sefirot (Chesed, Gevurah, Tiferet, Netzach, Hod, and Yesod) are collectively called the System of Justice in that they are responsive to human deeds, for even Chesed, which is pure kindness, applies only to the meritorious.

13. Keter is called Arich Anpin - Patient, because it represents unqualified mercy, which will only be fully realized in the world to come. (This gives the righteous the opportunity to acquire greater merit, and the wicked the chance to repent.) The six sefirot are called Zeir Anpin - Short Tempered, because they represent the qualified system of justice by which the world is presently being conducted.

14. Malchut is the medium for Divine providence through which the kingdom of G-d and his presence - Shechinah, will be realized and accepted by All. This sefirah has a dual function; it is a conduit that accepts mans good deeds and prayers, and responds by transmitting divine influence upon them.

15. The term Sefirot means Numbers - Mispar. The concept of sefirot can therefore be applied to many matters. Everything that exists can be divided into ten sefirot.

16. Scripture states: "All the hosts of heaven stand by Him to His right and to His left." The sages asked, "And are there right and left above? Rather, the right for virtue and the left for guilt." Therefore, a sefirah which influences Kindness to the worthy is allegorically considered "right" and one which influences Judgment upon the guilty is allegorically considered "left".

17. A diagram of the sefirot conveying this concept would therefore appear thus: Keter in the top center position, since it is the root of all. Under it, Chochmah to the right and Binah to the left, since in Binah descernments begin to arise. Under them Chesed to the Right and Gevurah to the left, with the median conduct of Tiferet centered below. Below them, Netzach to the right and Hod to the left, with the median conduct of Yesod centered below.

Under Yesod, in the center, Malchut which recieves from All.

18. This diagram is allegorically called the Ten Upright Sefirot - Esser Sefirot D'Yosher.

19. There is also a diagram of concentric circles in which Keter encompasses Chochmah, which in turn encompasses Binah, etc., with Malchut at its center. This diagram is called the Ten Sefirot of Circles - Esser Sefirot D'Igulim. It conveys principles in the development of the worlds one from the other, and indicates that the more essential the conduct, the more all encompassing it is. But, when the subject is the divine system of conduct, the quality of its various modes and their interrelationships, the diagram of the ten upright sefirot is used. (The GR"A states that the circular sefirot indicate general providence and the upright sefirot, individual providence).

20. Malchut is more severe than the six sefirot of Zeir Anpin, which represent the system of justice. For since Malchut is called "Righteous Judgment", it is more exacting. Only at times, through the merit of mankind does Malchut join Chesed (Kindness) resulting in Rachamim (Mercy).

21. A general conduct which is an expression of judgment, such as Malchut, is allegorically considered female. This is one reason that Malchut is often called Nukve (Female).

22. Binah is somewhat severe relative to Chochmah, since discernments begin to arise in it. Therefore, it too, is considered female. Accordingly, in kabbalistic terminology, when the judgmental aspect of a particular sefirah is mentioned, the feminine gender is used. For example, " Arich Anpin and his Female", refers to Keter, which is the quality of absolute mercy, and the potential judgment dormant in it. Gevurah and Hod, though they are expressions of judgment, are not generally considered female. This is because they are integral components in the reward and punishment of the System of Judgment - Zeir Anpin, and do not function independently of it.

23. The sefirot have both revealed and concealed aspects. The revealed is considered external, and the concealed, internal. An example of the concealed aspect is a kindness done in secrecy in which the kindness or goodness is not recognized, as stated in Proverbs: "Good is a revealed rebuke coming from a hidden love," and as stated in Talmud, "The recipient of a miracle does not recognize it as such."

24. Sometimes instead of Keter, Daat is enumerated amongst the sefirot. The GR"A explained that the inclusion of Keter reflects the inner aspect, while the inclusion of Daat, reflects the external aspect.

25. This is because the quality of Keter - Great Mercy is not presently revealed. It will only be fully realized in the world to come. This is indicated by the divine name E-H-EY-E-H - "I will be," in the future tense, meaning, "I am destined to be" - after the six thousandth year of creation. Since the conduct toward the world is preparatory to G-d's ultimate intent of benefiting all, Keter, though concealed, is its underlying and motivating force, as stated in the Talmud, "Everything that the Merciful One does is for the good." For this reason, Keter is only counted in respect to the hidden inner aspect but regarding the external aspect, Daat is counted instead, since it represents that minute revelation of Keter in this world, on a lesser level. It is, therefore, centered under Chochmah (which is free of Judgment) and Binah (in which discernments begin to arise) being a median conduct between them.

26. All that is revealed and is known to us of Keter is that this world is preparatory to its revelation in the world to come. Accordingly, Keter is the root of all present conducts since it was G-d's original intent to reveal Keter through them - "The last deed being in the first thought."

27. This explains the above statement that Keter is counted regarding the inner aspect, but regarding the external aspect, Daat is counted instead, and Keter is only considered the root. Keter is therefore called Ayn - Nothingness and Raysha D'Ayn - The Primal Nothingness, because we comprehend almost nothing of it. Accordingly, the GR"A states that, "revelation begins with Chochmah." The order of the sefirot would then be: Chochmah, Binah, Daat, Chesed, etc.

28. Thus, since the revealed aspect begins with Chochmah and Binah, they are called Father and Mother - Abba V'Ima, for since discernments begin to arise in Binah, it is considered female.

29. The sefirot can therefore be categorized into five general modes of conduct (Partzufim): Arich Anpin - Patient, for Keter, Abba - Father, for Chochmah, Ima - Mother, for Binah, Zeir Anpin - Short Tempered, for the six sefirot Chesed, Gevurah, Tiferet, Netzach, Hod, and Yesod (which collectively constitute the System of Justice, and, Nukvah - The Female, for Malchut.

Keter	Arich Anpin
Chochmah	Abba
Binah	Ima
Six sefirot	Zeir Anpin
Malchut	Nukvah

30. Sometimes the ten sefirot are categorized as the five kindnesses and the five severities. The five kindnesses are: Keter, Chochmah, Chesed, Tiferet, (since it inclines toward kindness), and, Netzach. The five severities are: Binah, Gevurah, Hod, Yesod (since it inclines toward judgment), and Malchut.

31. The six sefirot of Zeir Anpin are called

Vav Kitzvot (The Six Corners), corresponding to the six directions in the world: Chesed - corresponds to south, Gevurah - to the north, Tiferet - to the east, Netzach - to up, Hod - to down, and Yesod - to the west.

32. G-d formed all the limbs and organs of man corresponding to the supernal conducts. Each of man's limbs hints at a divine conduct. Since there are ten general sefirot, so too, in man, there are ten general corresponding parts: The Head - corresponds to the first three sefirot, The Skull and Membrane - to Keter, The Right Hemisphere of the Brain - to Chochmah, The Left Hemisphere of the Brain - to Binah, (The Cerebellum - to Daat) The Right Arm and Hand - to Chesed, The Left Arm and Hand - to Gevurah, The Torso - to Tiferet, The Right Leg and Foot, to Netzach, The Left Leg and Foot, to Hod, The Male Organ (which carries the sign of the Holy Covenant - Brit Kodesh) - To Yesod and the Glans (Ateret Habrit) - to Malchut.

33. Kabbalah sometimes refers to the sefirot by the names of their corresponding limbs in man. For example, Keter is called Gulgalta - Skull; Chochmah and Binah are called

Mochin - The Brains; Chesed is called The Right Arm, etc. Obviously, these names are allegorical. It should not, G-d Forbid, enter one's mind that any image or form exists, for this would certainly be an absolute error, constituting a complete denial of Torah.

The Beginning of Kabbalah Wisdom - Chapter 1

Chapter 2

Within which is explained the matter of the six hundred and thirteen (613) limbs and organs of man and their spiritual counterparts, as well as the subject of the Partzufim.

34. Above, the limbs of man and their spiritual counterparts were categorized in a general way. More specifically, the conducts are further subdivided. Every general sefirah of Keter contains ten sefirot, Keter of Keter, Chochmah of Keter, Binah of Keter, etc., until Malchut of Keter. So, also the general sefirah of Chochmah contains ten sefirot. Keter of Chochmah, Chochmah of Chochmah, etc., this principle applies to all the sefirot.)

35. Each particular sefirah contains ten further subdivisions. Keter of Keter contains Keter of Keter of Keter, Chochmah of Keter of Keter, Binah of Keter of Keter, etc., until Malchut of Keter of Keter. All the particular sefirot are subdivided in this manner.

36. Man's limbs and organs too, are subdivided corresponding to the subdivisions of their spiritual counterparts.

37. The Skull and it's Membrane which correspond to Keter, has ten components corresponding to the ten sefirot of Keter. Etz Chaim categorizes them as follows: The Skull corresponds - to Keter of Keter, The Right Ear - to Chochmah of Keter, The Left Ear - to Binah of Keter, (The Forehead - to Daat of Keter), The Right Eye - to Chesed of Keter, The Left Eye - to Gevurah of Keter, The Nose - to Tiferet of Keter, The Upper Lip - to Netzach of Keter, The Lower Lip - to Hod of Keter, The Tongue - to Yesod of Keter, The Mouth - to Malchut of Keter. Sefer Yetzira states that there are seven components in the head. These are called the Seven Gates or Orifices. According to the GR"A, they correspond to the seven sefirot: The Right Eye - to Chesed, The Left Eye - to Netzach, The Right Ear - to Gevurah, The Left Ear - to Hod, The Right Nostril - to Tiferet, The Left Nostril - to Yesod, and The Mouth - to Malchut.

38. Kabbalah sometimes refers to the subdivisions of Keter by the names of their corresponding parts in the head. For example: Peh - Mouth, refers to Malchut of Keter. This explains why Malchut is sometimes called Peh - Mouth, and sometimes Atara - Glans.

The term Peh - Mouth, may refer to the particular sefirah of Malchut of Keter, where as Atara - Glans, may refer to the general sefirah of Malchut. This principle applies to all the general and particular sefirot.

39. Each sefirah contains the three general modes of conduct: Pure Kindness, Pure Judgment, and the median conduct of Mercy. For example: the sefirah of Chesed contains Kindness of Chesed, Judgment of Chesed, and Mercy of Chesed. The sefirah of Gevurah contains Kindness of Gevurah, Judgment of Gevurah, and Mercy of Gevurah. This principle applies to all the sefirot.

40. Each of man's limbs contains three components corresponding to these three general modes of conduct: The Arms - which correspond to Chesed and Gevurah, each contain a hand, forearm, and upper arm. The Torso - which corresponds to Tiferet, contains the chest, heart area and navel area. The Legs - which corresponds to Netzach and Hod, each contain a thigh, calf and foot, etc.

41. The general modes of conduct as they exist in the sefirot are sometimes allegorically called by the names of their corresponding limbs in man: The Right Hand - corresponds to Kindness of Chesed, The Right Forearm - to Judgment of Chesed, The Right Upper Arm - to Mercy of Chesed, The Left Hand - to Kindness of Gevurah, The Left Forearm - to Judgment of Gevurah, The Left Upper Arm - to Mercy of Gevurah, The Chest - to Kindness of Tiferet, The Navel Area - to Judgment of Tiferet, The Heart - to Mercy of Tiferet, The Right Thigh - to Kindness of Netzach, The Right Calf - to Judgment of Netzach, The Right Foot - to Mercy of Netzach, The Left Thigh - to Kindness of Hod, The Left Calf - to Judgment of Hod, The Left Foot - to Mercy of Hod, etc.

42. Therefore, when the term Chazeh - Chest, is used in Kabbalistic literature, it refers to Kindness of Tiferet. Taboor - Navel, refers to Judgment of Tiferet, Right Hand to Kindness of Chesed, the Left Thigh to Kindness of Hod, etc...

43. Although Keter is absolute mercy, it is the root of all subsequent conducts which are preparatory to it, as stated, "The last deed was in the first thought," and therefore, possesses the potential qualities of Kindness, Judgment, and Mercy. In Keter these are called the Three "Heads" or "Beginnings."

44. These three heads constitute the highest of the ten sefirot of Keter. They are called Gulgalta - Skull, Moach - Brain, and Avira - Gaseous Membrane, that is, Keter of Keter, Chochmah of Keter, and the median conduct between them.

45. They are also called Ohr Kadmon - The Primal Light, Ohr Tzach - The Brilliant Light, and Ohr Metzuchtzach - The Radiant Light. The Zohar sometimes refers to Keter of Keter as Atika Kadisha - The Transcendent Holy One, and to Chochmah of Keter as Chochmah Stima'ah - The Hidden Chochmah, Mocha Stima'ah - The Hidden Brain, or Botzinah D'Kardenuta - The Black Flame. Because Kindness and Judgment are the more essential conducts (Mercy, being conditioning of the two) sometimes only they are enumerated. Furthermore, sometimes only one head is enumerated, since Judgment too, is ultimately for good.

46. The three elements Air, Water, and Fire, correspond to Mercy, Kindness, and Judgment, which are signified by the letters

Alef, Mem, and Shin. Alef - corresponds to Keter (or Daat), Mercy and Air, Mem - to Chochmah, Kindness and Water, and, Shin - to Binah, Judgment and Fire. Since Alef, Mem, and Shin are the source of all subsequent conducts, they are called "The Three Mothers."

47. There are a total of six hundred thirteen (613) conducts, corresponding to the six hundred thirteen parts in man: Two hundred forty-eight (248) organs and three hundred sixty-five (365) sinews.

48. The entire creation, consisting of both the upper spiritual worlds and the lower worlds, is made up of these six hundred thirteen (613) components, each of which has it's counterpart in man. Man, therefore, is a microcosm of the entire creation, the sum total of which can be conceived as one great stature.

49. Since each part of creation has its special quality, each receives a unique influence from G-d resulting in six hundred and thirteen (613) different influences. These differences do not arise in the giver, who is unchanging, but rather in the recipients due to their limitations.

50. Accordingly, a conduct which influences the entire Creation, is considered to consist of six hundred thirteen (613) components. However, one which influences a portion of creation consists of the number of corresponding parts in that portion.

51. The six hundred thirteen (613) components in their entirety are allegorically called "Man", and are considered to be one full stature - Partzuf. Only a conduct which influences all the components of Creation is called by this term.

52. There are five general Partzufim, each of which influences the entire Creation: Keter - Arich Anpin, Chochmah - Abba, Binah - Ima, Zeir Anpin - The System of Justice, and, Malchut - Nukvah.

53. The function of Malchut is to reveal G-d's kingdom and presence in the world. When this is fulfilled throughout Creation, Malchut is considered to be a complete stature - Partzuf. However, when man's transgressions cause the concealment of G-d's kingdom from this world as stated, "I will surely conceal my countenance on that day," Malchut cannot be considered complete, but rather a lesser aspect. This is comparable to the waxing and waning of the moon.

54. The apparent multiplicity of G-d's influence in the world is the result of the world's limitations and characteristics, and in no way reflect any limitations in Him. The divine influence given in them is in accordance with the number of their parts, even though one influence would be sufficient, as stated in Pirke Avot that the world could have been created with one utterance. Man too, was created with the number of his organs and sinews corresponding to the multiplicity of worlds, each organ corresponding to one world. Similarly, the soul of man has faculties corresponding to the organs of the body within which it resides. Because of this correlation of man, his soul, and the worlds, the sefirot are allegorically called "Man."

55. Therefore, due to this correlation, the worlds and conducts are sometimes allegorically called by the names of their corresponding organs in man.

56. The human soul, too, possesses six hundred and thirteen (613) parts, corresponding to the six hundred thirteen (613) organs.

57. So too, the Mitzvot of the Torah number six hundred thirteen (613), corresponding to the organs, parts of the soul, worlds, and conducts. When a person fulfills a Mitzva, he increases sanctity in those organs of his body which correspond to that Mitzva, which in turn causes a degree of perfection in the corresponding parts of his soul, and creation. When performed by an individual only that specific portion of Creation wherein his soul is rooted is affected. However, when performed communally, the Mitzvah affects the entire corresponding part of creation. Accordingly, when man takes the initiative in performing a Mitzvah, G-d responds in kind by bestowing blessings through the conduct which corresponds to that Mitzvah. Conversely, the transgression of a Mitzvah causes a blemish in all its corresponding parts.

58. Furthermore, all man's organs, natural characteristics, and life stages such as: Embryonic (Ibur), Infancy (Yenika),

Childhood (Katnut), and, Adulthood (Gadlut), etc. hint at great matters in G-d's conduct. These conducts are called by the names of the stages corresponding to them. Generally, everything that is found in man hints at G-d's hidden conduct toward Creation. In addition, this principle applies to the passage of time in general.

59. An alternate method of enumerating the two hundred forty-eight (248) conducts, corresponding to the two hundred forty-eight (248) organs is given in Etz Chaim: each of the three modes of conduct; Kindness, Judgment and Mercy, is subdivided to the fourth power as follows: Three times Three = Nine Three times Nine = Twenty Seven Three times Twenty Seven = Eighty One Three times Eighty One = Two Hundred Forty-Three The numerical value of the name AVRAM (אברם). With the addition of the five inner aspects, (i.e. the five Kindnesses) the total equals two hundred and forty-eight, the numerical value of the name AVRAHAM (אברהם).

Chapter 3

In which is explained the matter of the Divine names and the principles pertaining to them.

60. Midrash Rabba states, "G-d said to Moshe, "You wish to know my name? I am called according to my deeds. I may be called El Shaddai, Tzvaoth, Elokim or YHVH. When I judge the creatures, I am called Elokim, when I battle the wicked, I am called El Shaddai, and when I have mercy upon my world, I am called YHVH". The name YHVH always denotes the attribute of mercy, as stated, "YHVH, YHVH is a merciful and gracious G-d." This is the meaning of "I will be as I will be", that is "I will be called according to my deeds". (The sages stated that the names of the angels too, correspond to their mission, and differ accordingly.)

61. Likewise, the names of the Sefirot reflect their specific conduct, and differ accordingly.

62. The Ancients, therefore, mention ten unerasable names, corresponding to the vessels of the ten general sefirot through which G-d relates to his world, as follows;

Keter corresponds to Eheyeh Chochmah to Yah Binah to YHVH with the vowel points of Elokim (Daat to EHVE) Chesed to El Gevurah to Elokim Tiferet to YHVH Netzach to YHVH Tzvaoth Hod to Elokim Tzvaoth Yesod to Shaddai or El Chai and Malchut to Adonai

63. In addition, the name YHVH also alludes to all the ten Sefirot, as follows; The tip of the Yod corresponds to Keter, the body of the Yod to Chochmah the first Hey to Binah the vav to the six Sefirot of Zeir Anpin and the final Hey to Malchut.

64. YHVH indicates that G-d was, is, and will be, and is the source of all being. It alludes to the manner in which the world is presently conducted. Keter (or Eheyeh), though the underlying and motivating factor in the world, is exceedingly hidden, and will only be revealed in the world to come. For this reason, it is merely hinted at in the name YHVH, by the tip of the Yod.

65. Eheyeh represents Keter and Arich Anpin, which is great and unqualified mercy, whereas YHVH represents Tiferet and Zeir Anpin, which is the system of justice and qualified mercy. Yet Etz Chayim states that Eheyeh is a greater severity then YHVH. That is, since Eheyeh is presently withheld and will only be revealed in the world to come, the world as it is today receives greater mercy from YHVH than from Eheyeh which is almost entirely concealed, Its very concealment is its severity.

66. There are ten vowels, corresponding to the inner lights of the ten Sefirot. Each Sefira possesses the name YHVH with different vowel points, as follows;
Kamatz (אָ) for Keter,
Patach (אַ) for Chochmah,
Tzeirei (אֵ) for Binah,
Segol (אֶ) for Chesed,
Shvah (אְ) for Gevurah,
Cholem (אֹ) for Tiferet,
Chirik (אִ) for Netzach,
Koobootz (אֻ) for Hod,
Shoorook (אוּ) for Yesod,
And Malchut without vowels (א).

Know that the VOWELS are in every letter of the Aleph Bet. I used only the first letter Aleph, as an example.

67. The vessel of Daat is EHVH (אהו"ה) which

combines the first two letters (א"ה) of Eheyeh and the last two letters (ו"ה) of YHVH. The vowels of the YHVH of Daat which represents its inner light, are in accordance with the pronunciation of each particular letter, as follows; Cholem for the Yod (יֹ) Tzeirei for the Hey (הֵ) Kamatz for the Vav (וָ) and Tzeirei for the final Hey (הֵ) The name YHVH with these vowel points is called "The Ineffable Name" (שם המפורש).

68. The Divine names may be expanded by spelling out their individual letters as follows; Alef (אל"ף) Beit (בי"ת) Gimmel (גימ"ל) etc. The letters Hey (ה) and Vav (ו) each have three possible spellings; HY (ה"י) VYV (וי"ו) HA (ה"א) VAV (וא"ו) HH (ה"ה) VV (ו"ו) YHVH may therefore be expanded into several possible spellings depending on the variant spellings of the letters Hey (ה) and Vav (ו).

69. There are four general expansions of YHVH; The first is YOD HY VYV HY (יו"ד ה"י וי"ו ה"י) and is expanded with Yods. This is the name of 72-A"V (ע"ב) which is its numerical value. The second is YOD HY VAV HY (יו"ד ה"י וא"ו ה"י) and is expanded with Yods and an Aleph. This is the name of

63-SA"G (ס"ג) which is its numerical value. The third is YOD HA VAV HA (יו"ד ה"א וא"ה) and is expanded with Alephs. This is the name of 45-M"AH (מ"ה) which is its numerical value. The last is YOD HH VV HH (יו"ד ה"ה ו"ו ה"ה). This is the name of 52-B"AN (ב"ן) which is its numerical value. It is called Ban (ב"ן) though the proper grammatical form is Nav (נ"ב), the greater value preceding the lesser. This is to avoid the confusion of Av (ע"ב) with Nav (נ"ב).

72 ע"ב – יו"ד ה"י וי"ו ה"י

63 ס"ג – יו"ד ה"י וא"ו ה"י

45 מ"ה – יו"ד ה"א וא"ו ה"א

52 ב"ן – יו"ד ה"ה ו"ו ה"ה

70. The expansions of YHVH, (Av-72, Sag-63, Mah-45, and Ban-52) correspond to the five Statures (Partzufim) which are represented by the name YHVH; Av-72 corresponds to Keter and Chochmah, represented by the tip and body of the Yod (י). Sag-63 corresponds to Binah, represented by the first Hey (ה). Mah-45 corresponds to the six Sefirot of Zeir Anpin represented by the

Vav (ו). And Ban-52 corresponds to Malchut, represented by the final Hey (ה).

71. The letters Yod (י), Aleph (א), and Hey (ה), represent the three modes of conduct, Kindness, mercy and judgment. Av-72 represents Keter and Chochmah, because it is filled entirely with Yods, and is pure Kindness. Sag-63 is filled with Yods except for the Aleph in the Vav. This indicates that it is mostly kindness with a portion of mercy. It therefore represents Binah. The Aleph appears in the Vav of Sag-63 because the Vav as well represents the quality of mercy.

72. Mah-45 is merciful and inclines toward kindness (as does the Sefirah of Tiferet) because it is filled entirely with Alephs. It therefore corresponds to Zeir Anpin, the qualified system of justice. Ban-52 is Judgment. This is because it is filled with Heys and its Vav is empty. It therefore, represents Malchut, which is "Righteous Judgment" and may be severe.

73. Thus, Av-72 is entirely kindness, Sag-63 is kindness with a degree of mercy, Mah-45 is merciful and leans toward kindness, and Ban-52 is entirely judgment.

74. Each of these expansions, Av, Sag, Mah, and Ban may be subdivided as follows; Av of Av, Sag of Av, Mah of Av and Ban of Av etc. This principle applies to all four names.

75. These subdivisions may also be further subdivided as follows; Av of Av of Av, Sag of Av of Av, Mah of Av of Av, Ban of Av of Av. This applies to all the subdivisions.

76. Torah script is comprised of four elements. Cantillations, vowels, crownlets and letters, corresponding to Av, Sag, Mah, and Ban as follows; Av corresponds to Cantillations Sag to Vowels Mah to Crownlets and Ban to Letters. Sometimes the names Av, Sag, Mah, and Ban are called by these corresponding counterparts.

77. As Av, Sag, Mah, and Ban are subdivided, so too are these, as follows; Cantillations of Cantillations, Vowels of Cantillations, Crownlets of Cantillations, and Letters of Cantillations etc. This principle applies to all four elements.

78. Sometimes the letters and the crownlets are considered to be one, since they are connected when written in the Torah, so that only three elements are enumerated.

79. The name Eheyeh also has three extensions representing kindness, mercy, and judgment. The first is filled with Yods as follows; ALEPH--HY--YOD--HY (אל"ף ה"י יו"ד ה"י) and represents kindness of Eheyeh. It is called the name of 161 (קס"א) which is its numerical value. The second is filled with Alephs as follows; ALEPH--HA--YOD--HA (אל"ף ה"ה יו"ד ה"א) and represents mercy of Eheyeh. It is called the name of 143 (קמ"ג). The third is filled with Heys as follows; ALEPH--HH--YOD--HH (אל"ף ה"ה יו"ד ה"ה) and represents judgment of Eheyeh. It is called the name of 151 (קנ"א).

80. The name of Elokim also has three extensions representing kindness, mercy, and judgment. The first is filled with Yods as follows; ALEPH--LAMED--HY--YOD--MEM (אל"ף למ"ד ה"י יו"ד מ"ם) and represents an inclination toward kindness in Elokim. The second is filled with Alephs as follows; ALEPH--LAMED--HA--YOD--MEM (אל"ף למ"ד ה"ה יו"ד מ"ם) and represents an inclination toward mercy in Elokim. The third is filled with Heys as follows;

ALEPH--LAMED--HH--YOD--MEM (אל"ף למ"ד ה"ה יו"ד מ"ם) and represents the total judgment of Elokim.

81. The extended names may be further extended by spelling out each letter of the extension as follows; The Ineffable Name - Y-H-V-H Name of 72-Av - YOD--HY--VYV—HY Extension of Extension - YOD-VYV-DALET--HY-YOD--VYV-YOD-VYV—HYYOD This principle applies to all the divine names.

82. There is another aspect of the Divine names called Ribuah -squaring whereby after each consecutive letter the name reverts to its beginning, for example the square of YH-V-H is; Y (י) Y"H (י"ה) Y"H"V (י"ה"ו) Y"H"V"H (י"ה"ו"ה) The square of Shaddai is; SH (ש) SH"D (שד) SH"D"Y (שד"י) This principle applies to all the Divine names and indicates judgment. A squared name reflects the aspect of the "back".

83. The principle of Ribuah -squaring also applies to all the extended names, for example; the square of the name of 72-Av is; YOD-   (יו"ד)   YOD"HY-   (יו"ד ה"י)

YOD"HY"VYV- (יו"ד ה"י וי"ו)
YOD"HY"VYV"HY- (יו"ד ה"י וי"ו ה"י)

84. The letters of the divine names may also be arranged in all their possible combinations. This is called Tziruf -Combinations (צירוף). To illustrate, the name YOD--HEY--VAV (י'ה'ו) has six possible combinations corresponding to the six Sefirot, as follows; Chesed corresponds to Y"V"H (י'ו'ה) Gevurah to H"V"Y (ה'ו'י) Tiferet to V"Y"H (ו'י'ה) Netzach to Y"H"V (י'ה'ו) Hod to H"Y"V (ה'י'ו) and Yesod to V"H"Y (ו'ה'י) This order follows the principle that more essential quality takes precedence in the order of the letters. Chesed and Netzach, which are in the right column, begin with Yod, representing kindness. Gevurah and Hod, which are in the left column, begin with Hey, representing judgment. Tiferet and Yesod, which are in the middle column, begin with Vav, representing mercy. Since Chesed is a higher level of kindness than Netzach, the Vav representing mercy, precedes the Hey, which represents judgment. Netzach, being a lower level is the reverse. Since Gevurah is more severe in judgment than Hod, the Vav, representing mercy, precedes the Yod which represents Kindness. Hod, being less severe is the reverse. Since Tiferet inclines toward kindness, the Yod precedes the Hey. The reverse is true of Yesod.

85. A name consisting of four letters would normally have twenty-four possible combinations (צירופים), but since Y-H-V-H has two like letters, only twelve combinations are possible. Elokim, which has five letters, has one hundred twenty possible combinations. These are called "The one hundred twenty combinations of Elokim" (ק"כ צירופים דאלהים).

86. The general principle of combinations (צירוף) is that the closer the resemblance of the letters to the true configuration of the name, the more they indicate mercy, the more reversed they are, the more judgment.

87. The divine names may also be interwoven this is called Shiluv -weaving (שילוב) in which the letters of one name are coupled with those of another, in alternating order. For example, the names of Y-H-V-H and Adonai (A-D-N-Y) may be interwoven as follows;
    A.   Y'H'V'H   A'D'N'Y   = Y'A'H'D'V'N'H'Y (י'ה'ו'ה א'ד'נ'י = י'א'ה'ד'ו'נ'ה'י)

B.   A'D'N'Y   Y'H'V'H   = A'Y'D'H'N'V'Y'H (א'ד'נ'י י'ה'ו'ה = א'י'ד'ה'נ'ו'י'ה) The interweaving of two names indicates that two modes of Divine conduct are acting as one. The first letter of the weaving- Shiluv indicates which conduct is the more essential, to illustrate, in example:

(A) Y'H'V'H which represents mercy is the more essential whereas in example

(B) A'D'N'Y which represents Malchut and judgment is the more essential.

88. Just as the letters have numerical values, so do the vowels. The vowels are composed of lines and points. A point, which resembles the letter Yod, has the numerical value of ten. A line, which resembles the letter Vav, has the numerical value of six. The numerical values of the vowels are therefore;
Kamatz (אָ) 16 – Keter
Patach (אַ) 6 – Chochmah
Tzeirei (אֵ) 20 – Binah
Segol (אֶ) 30 – Chesed
Shvah (אְ) 20 – Gevurah
Cholem (אֹ) 10 – Tiferet
Cheerik (אִ) 10 – Netzach
Koobootz (אֻ) 30 – Hod
Shoorook (אוּ) 10 – Yesod
No Vowel – Malchut

89. There is a Divine name of seventy-two which is comprised of seventy-two three letter units. These are derived from the intertwining of the letters in three Biblical verses (Exodus 14:19 - 21) each of which contains seventy-two letters. The first letter of each of the seventy-two units are the letters of the first verse in their natural order. The middle letters of each of the units are the letters of the second verse, backwards, and the last letters, are the letters of the third verse, again in natural order. This name generally indicates the aspect of kindness. In Lurianic Kaballah "The name of seventy-two" usually refers to the extension of Y'H'V'H that has the numerical value of 72-Av (ע"ב) rather than this name.

90. The Divine names reflect G-d's actions toward the world. When in Scripture, one name is used and another is then introduced in its stead or added to it, this indicates a change of Divine influence toward the world. This comes about either through G-d's initiative or as a response to Mans deeds. When, for instance, the name Elokim is used and is then exchanged for Y'H'V'H, it indicates that the Divine influence changed from Judgment to Mercy.

91. G-d influences the world in accordance with its needs and as a response to Mans actions. When Man acts meritoriously, G-d responds with kindness and revelation, and if, G-d forbid, Man acts otherwise, G-d responds in kind. These different influences result from the needs of the recipients, and in no way indicate a change in the Giver, who is unchanging.

92. G-d influences the world in a multitude of ways, each of which has its own specific name. Every word in the Torah is a Divine name, the entire Torah being one great name of G-d.

93. Because each name represents a specific Divine action or aspect, it is important to have the proper intentions and concentration when uttering them during prayer. Ones prayers thus become more proper and acceptable before Almighty G-d, as stated in Scripture, "I will uplift him, for he knows my name". All this, of course, is in accordance with the righteousness of the individual and the degree of his understanding of these matters.

94. If a Divine conduct is destined to be revealed only in the world to come, the letters of its name are regarded as being hidden. However, if a conduct is presently revealed to a degree, the letters of its name are considered to be partially revealed.

95. Each Sefirah has many titles by which it is called corresponding to the various facets of its conduct.

96. Sefer Yetzirah categorizes the letters of the Hebrew alphabet into three categories. The first category is comprised of the letters Aleph (א) Mem (מ) and Shin (ש). These are called "The three Mothers" and correspond to the first three Sefirot as follows; Aleph (א) corresponds to air, and Keter (or Daat), Mem (מ) corresponds to water, and Chochmah, Shin (ש) corresponds to fire, and Binah. They also represent the horizontal "pipes" connecting the Sefirot.

97. The second category is comprised of the seven letters; They represent the vertical "pipes". Beit (ב) Gimmel (ג) Dalet (ד) Chaf (כ) Peh (פ) Raish (ר) Tav (ת) These are called the double letters since they can be read hard or soft as indicated by the presence or absence of a Dagesh (בגד כפרת). Though Raish is not written with a Dagesh, it is nonetheless pronounced hard or soft, and although Gimmel and Dalet may possess a Dagesh, their proper pronunciation has been lost. These seven double letters represent the seven lower Sefirot, Chesed, Gevurah, Tiferet, Netzach, Hod, Yesod, and Malchut, and are therefore pronounced hard and soft corresponding to Chesed (Kindness) and Rachamim (Mercy). The third category consists of the twelve remaining letters, which represent the diagonal "pipes". Hey (ה) Vav (ו) Zayin (ז) Chet (ח) Tet (ט) Yod (י) Lamed (ל) Nun (נ) Samech (ס) Ayin (ע) Tzaddik (צ) Kof (ק) The twenty-two letters represent twenty-two primary creative forces which are expressions of the ten Sefirot. All subsequent conducts and forces arise through combinations of these. There are two hundred, thirty-one possible two letter combinations. These are called "The two hundred, thirty-one Gates". Two hundred, thirty-one units are in forward order, indicating kindness, and two hundred, thirty-one units are in reverse order, indicating judgment.

Chapter 4

Which explains matters corresponding to the Sefirot and their interrelationships.

98. There are five general levels of the soul; Nefesh, Ruach, Neshamah, Chaya, and Yechidah. Each of these subdivided into five subsequent levels as follows; Nefesh of Nefesh, Ruch of Nefesh, Neshama of Nefesh, Chaya of Nefesh, and Yechida of Nefesh. This principle applies to all five general levels. These five levels correspond to the Sefirot as Follows: Nefesh corresponds to Malchut, Ruach to the six Sefirot of Zeir Anpin, Neshama to Binah, Chaya to Chochmah, and Yechidah to Keter.

99. Sometimes the Sefirot are allegorically called by the names of these corresponding levels of the soul.

100. There are many units of seven which correspond to the seven lower Sefirot through which the world is conducted. (The three upper Sefirot being presently concealed): Chesed corresponds to Wisdom Gevurah to Wealth, Tiferet to Offspring, Netzach to Life,

Hod to Dominion, Yesod to Peace, and Malchut to Grace.

101. There are seven directions: South corresponds to Chesed, North to Gevurah, East to Tiferet, Up to Netzach, Down to Hod, West to Yesod, and Center to Malchut. There are seven heavenly bodies: The moon corresponds to Chesed Mars to Gevurah The Sun to Tiferet Venus to Netzach Mercury to Hod Saturn to Yesod and Jupiter to Malchut. There are seven orifices in the head: The right eye corresponds to Chesed, The right ear to Gevurah, The right nostril to Tiferet, The left eye to Netzach, The left ear to Hod, The left nostril to Yesod, and the mouth to Malchut.

There are seven heavens:

Aravot (ערבות) corresponds to the three upper Sefirot, Keter, Chochmah, and Binah.
Ma'on (מעון) to Chesed,
Mechon (מכון) to Gevurah,
Zevul (זבול) to Tiferet,
Shechakim (שחקים) to Netzach and Hod,
Rakiah (רקיע) to Yesod,
Veelon (וילון) to Malchut.

There are seven days in the week:

Sunday corresponds to Chesed,
Monday to Gevurah,
Tuesday to Tiferet,
Wednesday to Netzach,
Thursday to Hod,
Friday to Yesod,
Shabbos to Malchut.

There are seven wildernesses within which the children of Israel sojourned: The wilderness of Eitam (מדבר איתם) corresponds to Chesed, The wilderness of Shor (מדבר שור) to Gevurah, The wilderness of Sin (מדבר סין) to Tiferet, The wilderness of Paran (מדבר פארן) to Netzach, The wilderness of Tzin (מדבר צין) to Hod, The wilderness of Kadmut (מדבר קדמות) to Yesod, The wilderness of Sinai (מדבר סיני) to Malchut. There are seven weeks of the Omer, seven years of the Shemitah, and seven Shemitot of the Yovel.

102. Accordingly there are seven metals which correspond to these Sefirot: Silver corresponds to Chesed, Gold to Gevurah, Bronze to Tiferet, Tin to Netzach, Lead to Hod, Mercury to Yesod, and Iron to Malchut. Everything that exists, has a correlation to one or more of the Sefirot. This includes animal, vegetable and mineral, as well as the sequence of time. Each millennium in history corresponds to a specific Sefirah. Since the mitzvot also correspond to the Divine conducts, each one affects its respective Sefirah.

103. Through the contemplation of three matters; the order of the worlds, the concept of time, and the nature of Man, one may arrive at an understanding of the Divine conducts. In Sefer Yetzirah these are called "World", "Year", and "Soul", (עש"ן or עולם שנה נפש).

Chapter 5

Within which is explained the matter of lights and vessels, the development of the worlds, the concept of enclothing, inner light, encompassing light, and rebounding light.

107. Although the Divine conducts are beyond grasp and definition, they are allegorically called "lights" (אורות) since there is nothing higher or more ethereal in empirical experience.

108. When reference is made to a "radiance" (הארה) of a particular light, this refers to a limited revelation of that Sefirah. 108B. The Sefirot develop one from the other in a descending order. This is called "The process of development" (השתלשלות). Keter gives rise to Chochmah, which gives rise to Binah etc., until Malchut, the one conduct necessitating the next. Through the contemplation of this process one can attain a deeper understanding of G-d's conduct toward the world. For example, though Gevurah is the conduct of judgment and punishment, we know that it arises from Chesed. It therefore is ultimately an act of kindness rather than a desire for vengeance on the part of G-d. Its true purpose is to deter Mankind from sin, as Scripture states, "G-d does it that people may fear Him" and "That those who remain will hear of it and fear." Furthermore, the individual experiencing the affliction also benefits, as stated, "Happy is the man afflicted of G-d." Also, "For G-d rebukes those He loves". and "As a man chastises his son" etc. But since the world cannot withstand absolute judgment, the intermediate conduct of mercy (Tiferet) arises. This principle applies to all the Sefirot, which develop one from the other in a similar fashion.

109. However, when one conduct precedes another in the process of development and the second conduct is the essential one, the prior conduct is considered to be preparatory to and as such stemming from the latter, essential conduct, "The last deed being the first in thought". Since this world and the fulfillment of the mitzvot in it, is preparatory to G-d's ultimate intent, it is considered to be secondary to, and therefore stemming from the world to come.

110. Because Keter, Chochmah, and Binah are the essential conducts of the world to come, the six Sefirot of the System of Justice-Zeir Anpin, which are preparatory to their ultimate fulfillment are thus considered to have arisen from them. Chochmah and Binah are the primary revealed conducts, (Keter being totally hidden) and are allegorically called Father- Abba and Mother- Imma, since they give rise to the conduct of the system of Justice, through which this world functions, as Scripture states, "For all His ways are Just."

111. Early writings sometimes refer to a primary conduct by the term "Cause" (עילה) and to a secondary conduct by the term "Effect" (עלול).

112. Another aspect of the Sefirot is that of "Enclothing" (התלבשות) whereby one conduct is concealed in and acts through a second conduct, which is the external expression of the inner, motivating one. The revealed conduct is considered to be the garment of the conduct concealed within it. Scripture thus states, "Good is a revealed rebuke coming from a hidden love", for example, a father who punishes or disciplines his child does so out of great love of the child and for his ultimate betterment, by correcting the negative characteristics he sees in him. If he did not care for the child, he would not be moved to discipline him, but to the casual observer it might seem a cruelty. The love and kindness of the father is enclothed, so to speak, within the external expression of punishment and discipline. 112B. Sometimes in G-d's relationship to Israel, the conduct of kindness is enclothed in that of judgment, for their ultimate good, as Scripture states, "As a man chastens his son, so does the L-rd your G-d chasten you". So too, concerning the suffering of the righteous, the sages stated, "Happy are the righteous who G-d did not countenance in this world". Scripture describes punishment as concealment of G-d's countenance, as it is written, "I shall surely conceal my countenance on that day".

113. The concept of enclothing may be further expanded, in that a specific part of one conduct may be enclothed in a specific part of another, all of which indicate sublime matters in G-d's conduct.

114. For example, Chesed of Arich Anpin (Keter) which is great mercy, is enclothed within Abba (Chochmah), Gevurah of Arich Anpin is enclothed in Imma (Binah), and

Tiferet, Netzach, Hod, and Yesod of Arich Anpin are enclothed in Zeir Anpin etc. as follows:

Arich Anpin

Chessed   Gevurah

Tiferet

Netzach   Hod

Yesod

Malchut

Enclothing Chochmah Bina Six Sefirot of Zeir Anpin Malchut Partzuf Abba Imma Zeir Anpin Nukvah the upper three Sefirot of Arich Anpin, are absolutely concealed and beyond grasp and as such cannot be enclothed in the lesser Sefirot. However, the general principles is that the lowest level of the higher aspect is enclothed in the highest level of the lower aspect, for example; the Malchut of Chesed is enclothed within the Keter of Gevurah etc. This principle applies to the Sefirot as well as the Partzufim and Worlds.

115. The concept of enclothing is related to that of lights and vessels in that a vessel limits and conceals the light and revelation within it in proportion to its density and/or lack of transparency. Light represents revelation (which is chesed) whereas vessels represent concealment (which is judgment and restriction) as Scripture states, "He set darkness as His hiding place".

116. Kabbalah speaks allegorically of three kinds of light; The first is revelation which is beyond grasp and cannot be contained within the vessel. It, therefore, is described as encompassing the vessel from a distance and is called, "Direct encompassing light" (אור מקיף הישר) The second is that light which is grasped and contained within the vessel. It is called, "Inner Light" (אור פנימי). The final light is called, "Rebounding encompassing light", (אור מקיף החוזר) in that it enters the vessel but cannot be contained within it, due to the limitations of the vessel. This light therefore rebounds and encompasses the vessel closely.

117. The GR"A applies this principle to the relationship between the upper three Sefirot and the seven lower Sefirot of Zeir Anpin and

Nukvah. Because discernments begin to arise in Binah, its light may be enclothed within the seven lower Sefirot as an inner light (Ohr Pnimi – אור פנימי). Nonetheless, due to the limitations of the recieving vessels, (rather than any limitation in Binah itself), only a fraction of its light is enclothed within them. Since Chochmah is not as absolute a kindness and mercy as Keter, its light may penetrate their vessels momentarily, but rebounds instantly due to their inability to grasp it. It therefore represents the Encompassing Rebounding light (Ohr Makif Hachozer – אור מקיף החוזר). Keter is absolute and unqualified Kindness and Mercy and therefore it represents the Direct encompassing light (Ohr Makif Hayashar – אור מקיף הישר). It cannot be grasped at all within the seven lower Sefirot and as such, is beyond comprehension and exceedingly hidden.

118. Each Partzuf possesses five distinct qualities: three types of light; The encompassing direct light (Ohr Makif Hayashar – אור מקיף הישר), The encompassing Rebounding light (Ohr Makif Hachozer – אור מקיף החוזר), and the inner light (Ohr Pnimi – אור פנימי), and two aspect of vessels; the internal (פנימי), and the external (חיצוני).

The Beginning of Kabbalah Wisdom - Chapter 5

Chapter 6

Within which is explained the world of Tohu-Chaos, the world of Tikkun- Repair, The connection of the three upper Sefirot with the seven lower ones, Yisroel Saba, Tevunah, The seven Repairs, and the thirteen Repairs of the Beard.

119. The Sages noted, "At first the world was created through the attribute of Judgment, G-d saw that the world could not withstand this so He joined the attribute of Mercy to it." For this reason, the Torah begins with the name Elokim (אלהים), signifying Judgment, and only later, in order to soften its nature, the name Y'H'V'H, which signifies mercy is used, as is written "On the day that Y'H'V'H Elokim made Earth and Heaven". The primary and fixed nature of the world is that of Judgment since it was originally created through this attribute. Mercy, however, is added to the world to soften its natural harshness in accordance to the degree of Mans righteousness. Conversely, to the degree of his transgressions, it is withdrawn, resulting in a regression to its primary nature. [A. The nature of the world (HaTeva - Nature = 86) is basically severe since its source is in the divine name Elokim = 86.] B. This is the concept of Shituf - Joining in which two conducts act in partnership thus tempering each other.

120. As explained previously the name of Ban-52, indicates absolute judgment, and the name of 45, mercy. As such the Sefirot were first ordered through this aspect of Ban-52. Because the conduct of judgment in and of itself could not bring about G-d's ultimate intent in Creation, Flaws resulted. 1 "Flaws Resulted" - Intentionally in order to bring about the Sitra Achara - which would create the possibility of free choice thus making man a free agent. These flaws are allegorically described as the shattering and fall of the vessels. This stage of creation is referred to as the World of Nekudim -Points or Tohu - Chaos, during which the light and revelation intended for the ultimate good was withdrawn. This is alluded to in the verse "And these are the kings that reigned in the land of Edom before there reigned any king of the children of Israel." Edom -(red), indicates Judgment alluding to the named of Ban-52, the World of Tohu- Chaos. Each of the kings of Edom indicates one of the Sefirot of Tohu as follows:

Bela ben Beor – Daat.

Yovav – Chesed.

Chusham – Gevurah.

Hadad ben Badad – Tiferet.

Samlah – Netzach and Hod.

Shaul – Yesod.

Baal Chanan ben Achbor - Malchut.

Hadar - Concerning each these kings (with the exception of Hadar,) Scripture states their demise, thus alluding to the shattering of their vessels. This was not the case with Hadar - Malchut, for at that stage the attributes of Mercy, alluded to by the name of 45 was introduced in order to bring about the eventual Tikkun - Repair. What is meant here by death is not a total cessation but rather a descent to a lesser state of being as explained in the Zohar, Idra Raba "They were nullified and withdrew from that state of being, not that they were totally nullified but rather, whenever there is a descent from a higher to a lower level, it is allegorically considered a death." This concept is also explained in Zohar on the verse "And the king of Egypt died." Such is also the case whenever a person falls from his level of spiritual awareness. This concept of death applies when an inner aspect is withdrawn from an external one, the inner aspect symbolizing the soul and the external, the body. Therefore, when a conduct descends to a lower level within which the higher aspect is no longer enclothed, it is considered similar to death. The intellectual Sefirot of Tohu were not shattered. This is why Esav's - (Tohu) head is buried in Maarat HaMachpela.

121. After the shattering of these vessels, the aspect of Mercy- Rachamim, which is the conduct of Mah-45, was introduced and superimposed upon that of 52, in order to soften its severity and to lead to the eventual rectification and complete goodness which is G-d's ultimate intent in Creation. This process is called the world of Tikkun - Repair (התיקון עולם).

122. This repair, comes about through the union of Mah-45 & Ban-52 and is a gradual process which is affected by three factors; mans deeds, G-d's Supernal intervention, and the various stages of time in G-d's ultimate plan.

123. The principle of rectification also applies to the six sefirot of Zeir Anpin.
Through the merit of Mankind the three upper Intellectual Sefirot (Keter, Chochmah, and Binah) - great mercies, are invested within Zeir Anpin, thus affecting its maturation, resulting in Goodness and Blessing to the world. This is alluded to in the verse "Do not come in Judgment with your servant." (Mishpat = Justice = Zeir Anpin). This concept is also called Shituf- Joining. Keter, Chochmah, and Binah join Zeir Anpin.

124. However, when Binah is joined with Zeir Anpin, only Malchut of Binah, its tenth part, does so. It therefore receives a distinct designation as a separate Stature- Partzuf containing ten sefirot, and is called Tevunah (תבונה).

125. The three lower Sefirot of Tevunah, Netzach, Hod, and Yesod, which represent Kindness, Judgment, and Mercy, become invested as an Ohr Pnimi -inner light within the six sefirot of Zeir Anpin. Each of these sefirot consists of ten subdivisions, totaling 90 - the numerical value of the letter Tzaddik (צ).

126. Chesed, Gevurah, and Tiferet of Tevunah become an Ohr Chozer- Rebounding encompassing light, relative to Zeir Anpin. They too consist of ten subdivisions totalling 30, the numerical value of the letter Lamed (ל). The four upper Sefirot of Tevunah; Keter, Chochmah, Binah, and Daat, are Ohr Yashar - a Direct encompassing light from a distance, in relation to Zeir Anpin, which consists of a total of 40 subdivisions, the numerical value of the letter Mem (מ). All these aspects together make up the word TZELEM - (צלם) - Image.

127. In that Mans nature and characteristics were created in a manner which hints at the supernal Conducts, his soul consists of three components corresponding to TZELEM; The Neshama which is enclothed within him, The Chaya which encompasses above him closely, and the Yechidah which encompasses above him at a distance. This is the meaning of the verse "G-d made man in his IMAGE - TZELEM." Kabbalah sometimes refers to the corresponding Supernal Conducts by these names. 3 In actuality the soul consists of 5 levels (NaRaN"CHaY)

128. When Mankind is meritorious, there is a Shituf- Joining of Tevunah itself with Zeir Anpin, however when this is not the case, only Malchut of Tevunah, which is its tenth part joins Zeir Anpin. It is considered to be a distinct Partzuf -Stature and is called the Second Tevunah 4 .(תבונה שניה) Malchut of Malchut of Binah

129. The concept of Tevunah only applies to the joining of Binah with Zeir Anpin. Otherwise, Binah is simply refered to as Imma.

130. If mankind acheives greater merit, then a Joining - Shituf is effected between the level of Malchut of Chochmah, and Zeir Anpin. This too becomes a distinct Partzuf called Yisrael Saba (ישראל סבא), and similarly to Tevunah, joins in an aspect of Tzelem, that is, one inner light and two encompassing ones. But when mankind is not so meritorious, only the Malchut of Yisroel Saba influences Zeir

Anpin. This is called the Second Yisroel Saba (ישראל סבא שני), and also influences Zeir Anpin through the three aspects of Tzelem. Certainly, the influence of Chochmah is higher than that of Binah and requires greater merit. 5 Malchut of Malchut of Chochmah.

131. Daat may also affect Zeir Anpin and with even greater merit an influence from Keter may be achieved.

132. Essentially Zeir Anpin consists of 6 Sefirot; Chesed, Gevurah, Tiferet, Netzach, Hod, and Yesod, but because the merits of Mankind (MiLemata LeMaala – from below to above), and Rectification (MiLeMaala Lemata – from above to below), This temporal world also recieves influence from Chochmah, Binah, and Daat or Keter by their joining with Zeir Anpin thus increasing its stature to a conduct of ten Sefirot. Zeir Anpin is then considered to possess a Keter, Chochmah and Binah in addition to its essential Sefirot. This matter applies after Tikkun.

133. For this reason Zeir Anpin is generally considered to consist of 6 Sefirot for being that they preceded Tikkun they are essential and constant, whereas that which issues after Tikkun may change.

134. Chochmah, Binah, and Daat are called Intellect. Therefore, their addition to the conduct of Zeir Anpin is regarded as an influence of "Intellect". Likewise, just as Man's body is of this world and his soul, which transcends the world, resides in his brain, so too the joining of a higher conduct to a lower one is allegorically called an "Influence of Intellect".

Binah   Chochmah
          Daat

135. It is written, "May the power of G-d be magnified." When G-d, Blessed Be He, influences kindness, miracles and goodness towards the world this is allegorically considered to be a magnification of his power since we only speak of His actions, as mentioned above. Conversely, when G-d conducts the world with severity and withholds his influence and revelation, His name is not magnified but is rather diminished. This is called Katnut -Smallness or Immaturity. (Symbolized by the stages of childhood in human developement.) When

Binah joins and influences the world, it is called Gadlut Rishon - The First or Initial Maturation (Magnification) And when there is a further joining and influence of Chochmah, it is called Gadlut Sheini - The Second or Greater Maturation.

136. All the stages of life, Embryonic, Infancy, Childhood, Adulthood etc., hint at the divine conducts. The Embryonic stage, in which the embryo is concealed and totally dependent on its mother for sustenance, is comparable to a time of severity, in which the world lacks merit and divine revelation as stated, "I will surely hide My face on that day". It then is sustained sole through G-d's grace and the merit of the Patriarchs. This connection between the Embryonic stage and G-d's conduct is hinted at in the scriptural verse, "Just as you know not what is the way of the wind or how the bones grow in the womb". The Egyptian bondage as well as our present state of exile constitutes such a period. The state of the Jewish people during the exodus was comparable to infancy marking the birth of the nation. However since they did not yet receive Torah and Mitzvot, they lacked meritorious actions. In like manner there is a relationship between all of Mans life stages and G-d's actions.

137. Revelation begins with Chochmah and therefore all subsequent conducts are included potentially within it. These are the thirty-two general paths or ways of G-d alluded to in the verse, "Please make your ways known to me". Sefer Yetzirah therefore states that, "G-d engraved Thirty-Two wondrous paths of Chochmah", which correspond to the 10 sefirot and the 22 letters of the Hebrew Alpha-Bet, each of which indicates a seperate conduct.

138. Keter also influences Zeir Anpin through its two heads, Keter of Keter which is the Gulgalta- Skull, and Chochmah of Keter which is the Mocha -Brain.

139. There are seven influences- Tikkunim of Keter of Keter, the first head, which are allegorically refered to by the following terms:

    A. Skull- Gulgalta.

    B. The Crystal Dew- Talla D'Bdulcha.

C. Gaseous Membrane- Krooma D'Avirah.

D. The White Hair of the Head- Amar Nakki.

E. The Primordial Desire or Will- Ra'ava D'Ra'avin (which is revealed in prayer) also allegorically called "The Forehead of Will"- Metzach Ratzon.

F. Conscious Supervision- Ashgacha P'Kicha- Also called- The Eye- Aiyna.

G. The Two Nostrils- Trayn Nukvin D'Pardashka - Also called- The Nose- Chutmah All these terms indicate types of influences from Keter of Keter and as such are exceedingly hidden. They are collectively called The Seven of The Skull- Shiva D'Galgalta.

140. Chochmah of Keter, which is the second head, and is called, The Hidden Brain- Mocha Stima'ah, possesses thirteen influences- Tikkunim that influence downward. These are the thirteen attributes of Mercy which were given over to Moshe. They are:

1. E-L - Benevolent G-d.

2. Rachum – Compassionate.

3. V'Chanun - and Gracious.

4. Erech - Long (slow).

5. Apayim - Suffering (to anger).

6. V'Rav Chessed - and Abounding in Kindness.

7. V'Emet - and Truth.

8. Notzer Chesed - He Preserves Kindness.

9. L'Alaphim - for two thousand generations.

10. Noseh Avon - Pardoning Iniquity

11. VaPeshah - and Transgression.

12. V'Chata'a - and Sin.

13. V'Nakeh - and He Cleanses.

141. There are thirteen corresponding phrases in Micha (7:18-20). They are:

1. Mi E-l Kamocha - Who is a G-d like you.
2. Nos'eh Avon - Who pardons iniquity.
3. V'Over Al Peshah - and forgives transgression.
4. L'She'erit Nachalato - for the remnant of His Heritage.
5. Lo Hechezik La'ad Apo - He does not maintain His wrath forever.
6. Ki Chafetz Chesed Hu - for He desires to do Kindness.
7. Yashuv Yerachamenu - He will again show us mercy.
8. Yichbosh Avonoteinu - He will suppress our iniquities.
9. Vetashlich BiMtzulot Yam Kol Chatotam - and you will cast all their sins into the depths of the sea.
10. Titen Emet L'Yaakov - Give truth to Jacob.
11. Chesed L'Avraham - Kindness to Abraham
12. Asher Nishbata LaAvoteinu - which you swore to our fathers.
13. M'Yimei Kedem - from the days of old.

142. Notzer Chesed is called the upper Mazal and V'Nakeh is called the lower Mazal and as such they sometimes influence jointly. These two are the more essential of the thirteen attributes. They are called Mazal in that they are good influences which descend from G-d and are non-reactive to human deed, as is written, "I will be gracious to whomever I will be gracious". The word MAZAL is related to Nozel which means to flow down. Concerning this the sages stated "Procreation, Health, and Livelihood are not determined by merit, but rather by Mazal.

143. As stated previously the characteristics of Man hint at the supernal conducts. So too the human beard hints at these attributes. They are therefore called, "the thirteen influences of the beard - Yud Gimel Tikunei Dikna". Because hair is tubular, influence from the brain is drawn down through them. Furthermore, in that they are very narrow this influence is exceedingly constricted and hidden. This is so because the influence comes through Chochmah of Keter which is somewhat less merciful in comparison to Keter of Keter. As a result, it is possible to perceive matters pertaining to a person's thoughts by observing his hair. However, these matters are very hidden and only perceptible to those who are greatly versed in physiognomy (Chochmat HaPartzuf) as explained in Zohar.

Chapter 7

Within which is explained the joining & union of Mercy - (Rachamim) with Judgment - (Din), the six sefirot of Zeir Anpin with Malchut, G-d, Blessed be He with the worlds, & the feminine waters with the masculine waters.

144. The conduct of Zeir Anpin is also termed Israel (ישראל), and the conduct of Malchut is also termed Rachel (רחל). Zeir Anpin possesses a secondary quality termed Jacob (יעקב), and Malchut too possesses a secondary quality termed Leah (לאה)

145. The GR"A explains that the reason for these two aspects of Rachel and Leah in Malchut is because there are two aspects of G-d's Kingdom. One aspect is our acceptance of the yoke of his kingdom willingly and faithfully without the force of miracles, as stated, "Say Malchuyot before me in order that you coronate me as your King." This is the ultimate goal of our service of G-d and is termed Rachel. The second aspect is the revelation of His Kingdom by force of miracles as in the exodus from Egypt and as will be in the time to come. This aspect displays G-d's splendor, yet he is called, "Humble" for, "Wherever His greatness is, so is His humility." This is termed Leah. There are also two aspects of Zeir Anpin. Our adherence and acknowledgment of Gd's existence on the basis of faith, is termed Jacob - Yaakov, that is, that we recognize and believe that G-d is the source of all reward and punishment, though it is not readily apparent. The second aspect represents the revelation of G-d as the source of everything, and is termed Israel - Yisrael. The essential quality in Zeir Anpin is that of - Yisrael - revelation, while the essential aspect in malchut is that of Rachel - acceptance.

146. As is known, Avraham Avinu personifies the attribute of Chesed - Kindness, Yitzchak Avinu that of Gevurah - Judgment, and Yaakov Avinu, the median attribute of Tiferet - Mercy. Chesed is therefore sometimes termed Avraham, Gevurah is termed Yitzchak, and Tiferet is termed Yisrael or Yaakov. Since the generation of the exodus lived in a miraculous fashion, unique to history, the aspect of Leah is sometimes termed Dor HaMidbar - The generation of the Exodus.

147. The world is generally conducted through the attribute of Malchut which is more severe than Zeir Anpin. As such it is called Nukvah - Female, and represents an exacting Judgment. Zeir Anpin, which is the conduct of Justice, Represents a more lenient, merciful judgment. If the world is meritorious, Zeir Anpin joins with Malchut affecting Goodness. If not, Zeir Anpin seperates, and the world is conducted solely through the severity of Malchut. It all depends on Mans deeds. This is in accordance with the statement "The world was originally created with judgment. G-d, seeing that it would not withstand, added the quality of Mercy".

148. This is the matter of Zivug - Joining mentioned in Kabalistic literature such as the Zivug -joining of Zeir Anpin to Malchut, that is, the superaddition of the mercies of Zeir Anpin to the Judgment of Malchut. This is accomplished through the prior joining of the conducts of Chochmah and Binah with those of Zeir Anpin. As a result, Zeir Anpin gains a greater degree of Mercy and in turn joins with Malchut affecting kindness and goodness towards the world.

149. Included in the function of Malchut is to manifest G-d's Kingdom in the world & to sanctify His great name. Since Man was given free choice, it is his responsibility, through his deeds, to lovingly receive the yoke of G-d's Kingdom and properly serve him, thereby Sanctifying & Glorifying His name. This causes rectification throughout all worlds and draws down G-d's Shechinah - Presence and Sanctity in them, thus bringing about the optimal revelation of His Kingdom. The reverse is true if man acts rebelliously. In this respect, all worlds may be considered branches of Malchut, since it reveals G-d's Kingdom which is G-d's ultimate goal in creation. This is accomplished through the Union between the mercies of Zeir Anpin & The Judgment of Malchut (Nukvah) and is determined by the deeds of man.

150. The principle of Zivug - Union implies a joining of a conduct of Mercy with one of Judgment, and represents the Union of the names of 45 & 52. As such, Zivug is not limited to Zeir Anpin and Nukvah but applies to other conducts as well. 150b. The joining of two conducts results in a third median conduct which though a synthesis of the two, is uniquely different from them. [for example,

Oxygen with Hydrogen is water] This Concept is explained in Nefesh HaChaim, "Concerning the concept of Zivug; certainly, it is to be taken allegorically and alludes to union in spiritual terms. It is similar to a person who combines two Ideas in his mind arriving at a third.

Though a synthesis of the two, it is never the less new and different.

151. The basis of Zivug is the revelation and connection of the Creator to His worlds or the lack thereof, all of which depends on the deeds of Man.

152. There are four spiritual Worlds: Emanation:

    Atzilut Creation.

    Briah Formation.

    Yetzirah Action.

    Asiyah Doing.

The first and highest of the created worlds is Briah, since Atzilut, being an emanation of G-d is in a sense an extension of Him. The world of Briah is Feminine relative to Atzilut. Before the sin of Adam, the two were in a state of Zivug, which is the union of the Male & Female aspect, in which the one gives & the other receives. Adams sin resulted in their separation. This is the meaning of the statement in the Zohar that the Matronita separated from her husband. 152b. Briah is called Matronita - Mother since it is the highest and first of the created worlds which issue from her. Similarly, the Torah often compares the relationship of G-d and the Jewish people to that of Man and Wife. 1 Chochmah corresponds to Atzilut, Binah corresponds to Briah, Zeir Anpin corresponds to Yetzirah, Nukvah corresponds to Asiya.

153. The union and joining of Mercy with Judgment, or the connection of G-d with the worlds, depends on and is initiated by the merits of Mankind. This union in turn causes a precipitation of influence from above, as scripture states, "Truth sprouts from the earth (i.e. from below) and G-d will give goodness (i.e. responding from above)". The merit and awakening from below is called Mayim Nukvim - Feminine Waters whereas the influence from above which follows, is called Mayim D'Churin - Masculine Waters.

154. The world of Briah which is the Matronita is sometimes called Malchut.

155. When as a result of Man's deeds Malchut is in a diminished state and the Shechinah is concealed from Mankind, it is similar to a solitary point. Conversely, when the Shechinah is revealed throughout the 613 components of creation, Malchut is considered to be a complete Partzuf - Stature comprising 613 parts. There are several aspects in man that correlate to the various states of Malchut. The Glans alludes to Malchut in its diminished state. 155b. The state in which Adam and Eve were originally attached to each other back to back, alludes to Malchut in a fuller state affecting the entire creation as a Partzuf - Stature. Their separation and relating face to face as well as their previous state of attachment parallel the union and separation of the world of Briah - Matronita which is the world of separation - Olam HaPirud with that of Atzilut. Furthermore, there are many profound concepts which are alluded to in these matters.

The Beginning of Kabbalah Wisdom - Chapter 7

Chapter 8

Within which is explained the stages of conduct until eternity, Adam Kadmon and his Branches, and the emanations of his ears, nose, and mouth, the world of Bundles, Tzimtzum, and the Ray.

156. There are two general stages in time; This world - Olam HaZeh and the World to Come - Olam HaBah. This world will endure six millennia corresponding to the divine conducts, Chesed, Gevurah, Tiferet, Netzach, Hod, and Yesod, in that order. The era of Moshiach, which ushers in the periods of Malchut is a transitional stage. It will begin during the latter part of the sixth millennium (and will conclude with the resurrection of the dead). The seventh millennium marks the beginning of the world to come and corresponds to Malchut. It will be of a higher order than the preceding six. During this stage the world ceases to exist in its present form and will be in a state of desolation for 1000 years, as scripture states "A song for the day of Sabbath". That is, a Sabbath of eternal rest. During this period the righteous will hover over the world like the ministering angels.

The eighth millennium, corresponding to Binah will be higher still and represent the renewal of the world and the final and eternal resurrection, as stated "The Holy One Blessed Be He will renew His world after the seventh millennium". The ninth and tenth millennia correspond to Chochmah and Keter and represent higher levels. The conclusion of the tenth millennium marks the beginning of the eternal conduct which transcends time, and represents the ultimate goodness. However, since death ceases from the seventh millennium on, these stages are also considered to be aspects of the eternal conduct.

157. The eternal conduct, following the conclusion of the tenth millenium is totally beyond our comprehension. It is the culmination and ultimate purpose of all creation and is called Adam Kadmon - Primordial Man; Adam - Man, because it embodies and fulfills all 613 components of creation and is therefore a full stature. Kadmon - Primordial, because it is Gd's original and essential intent in the creation of the world, all other conducts being merely preparatory to its fulfillment as stated "The last deed was first in thought".

158. Any intended conduct which is preceded by one or more preparatory ones is considered to be their cause. Therefore, all conducts from the beginning of creation to the conclusion of the tenth millennium are considered to be caused by and branches of Adam Kadmon.

159. Within the framework of time, there are six basic stages or branches. The first stage was the creation of the world through the name of 52-Ban, representing strict judgment. This was also the world of Tohu - Chaos or Nekudim - Points. The second stage was the introduction of the name 45-Mah representing mercy. This is the world of Tikkun - Repair. The last four stages are the seventh through tenth millennia of the world to come. All these stages are branches of Adam Kadmon.

160. The four expansions of the name -
$$Y\text{-}H\text{-}V\text{-}H$$
correspond to the elements of Torah Script and the millennia as follows:
    AV-72
    SAG-63
    MAH-45
    BAN-52

Taamim – Cantillations Nekudim – Vowels Tagin – Crownlets Otiyot – Letter Tenth Millennium Ninth, Eighth, and Seventh Millennium Tikkun Tohu

161. As previously stated each of the four expansions of Y-H-V-H have lower subdivisions which correspond to the four elements of Torah script. AV is divided into the cantillations, vowels, crownlets and letters all of which pertain to the tenth millennium. In SAG, cantillations which is the first of its four subdivisions, corresponds to the ninth, eighth and seventh millennia as follows: The upper cantillations (those appearing above a letter) correspond to the ninth millennium. The middle cantillations (those appearing next to a letter such as a "Sof Pasuk") correspond to the eighth millennium and the lower cantillations (those appearing under a letter) correspond to the seventh millennium. The remaining three subdivisions which are the vowels, crownlets and letters of SAG join with and influence this world, i.e., the names of MAH - 45 and BAN - 52. The four subdivisions of MAH – 45 correspond to Tikkun, and the four subdivisions of BAN - 52 correspond to Tohu.

162. Since the ninth, eighth and seventh millennia correspond to the upper, middle and lower cantillations they are sometimes alluded to by these terms.

163. The six above mentioned conducts are branches of Adam Kadmon. They are allegorically called after those areas of the head from which influence emanates. Because the conduct of AV (the tenth millennium) is above comprehension it is allegorically compared to the skull (which is sealed), and its hair. The remaining conducts correspond to five areas of the skull from which influence emanates. They are: the eyes – sight the ears – hearing the nose – smell the mouth - speech. Under special conditions, influence may emanate from the forehead, which constitutes the fifth area, such as the rays of light which emanated from the forehead of Moshe Rabbeinu, or as is stated in Midrash concerning Pinchas that during a state of divine inspiration his face shone like flames of fire. The hair comes out from the skull, which is sealed, yet originates in the brain, though its connection with the brain is not physically apparent.

164. These five branches or conducts which emanate from Adam Kadmon may therefore be ordered as follows; The ninth millennium corresponds to the ears and hearing. The eight millennium corresponds to the nose and smell. The seventh millennium corresponds to the mouth and speech. The name of 52-Ban which is World of Tohu and the conduct of Judgement, corresponds to the eyes and sight. The name of 45-Mah which is the world of Tikkun and the conduct of Mercy, corresponds to the radiance of the forehead. 7 Just as the radiance of the forehead is a supernatural occurance and is not part of the essential nature of a human being, so too the influence of Mercy was superadded to the primary nature of the world, which is Judgement.

165. We see from this that the temporal conducts which are branches of the eternal one of Adam Kadmon may therefore be catagorized in this fashion: Tenth Millenium - General name of 72 - General cantillations - above comprehension Ninth Millenium - Name of 72 of 63 first aspect - upper cantillations of vowels - hearing - ears Eight Millenium - Name of 72 of 63 second aspect - middle cantillation of vowels - smell - nose

Seventh Millenium - Name of 72 of 63 third aspect - lower cantillation of vowels - speech – mouth Judgment of this world - General Name of 52 - General Letters - Sight - Eyes The superaddition of Tikkun to this world - General name of 45 - general crownlets - Radiance of the Forehead.

166. Gemara, Sanhedrin states that in the seventh millennium the, "Holy One Blessed Be He will make wings for the Righteous". Though this will be a period of great spirituality, the world will not yet be renewed. This stage is called the World of Akudim - The Bundled World, in which the lights of all ten Sefirot are bundled together in only one vessel comparable to a mouth. [These lights emanate from the "mouth" of Adam Kadmon.] The concept of the spreading forth and withdrawal of the lights which is called "Going and not Going" (Mati V'Lo Mati - מטי ולא מטי) also applies to this level.

167. However in regard to the remaining millennia (eighth, ninth and tenth) in which G-d renews his world, only lights exist and there is no concept of "vessels" whatsoever.

168. The world of Tikkun is called the world of "Streaks" (Olam HaBrudim). Since the intended goal of creation is to achieve Olam Habba - The world of Akudim, conceptually the order of these stages is Olam Adudim, Nekudim and Brudim. However in order to bring this about the order in time is reversed so that the world of Tohu (Nekudim) precedes that of Tikkun (Brudim) which precedes and brings about G-d's ultimate intention Olam Habba (Akudim). This is in keeping with the statement "The first in thought is the last in deed".

169. Adam Kadmon which is the eternal conduct, also possesses ten sefirot. Malchut of Adam Kadmon is considered to be a distinct partzuf - Stature and is called Atik - Ancient or Reisha D'Lo ItYada - The Unknowable Head.

170. The fulfillment of every Mitzva leaves an eternal impression and is established for ever. The culmination of all the Mitzvot, will cause complete repair and absolute perfection - The Eternal Conduct. Atik is the link between the temporal and the eternal. It uplifts the deeds of this world and establishes them for eternity.

171. Malchut of Adam Kadmon, i.e. Atik, is enclothed within the conduct of Keter (Arich Anpin). Through this the absolute Chessed of Adam Kadmon becomes the inner, guiding force of Arich Anpin. The seven lower sefirot of Atik become enclothed within Arich.

172. As previously mentioned there are seven repairs of Keter of Keter called Tikunei D'Galgalta - the seven repairs of the skull. These arise from the conduct of Atik through the enclothing of its seven lower sefirot within Arich. As a result, Atik is enclothed within the whole of Atzilut.

173. When considering the world of Atzilut in general, Atik and Arich are not differentiated from each other but act together as aspects of Keter of Atzilut. As such, they are called Atika Kadisha since "He is called according to his deeds", as mentioned above. Early Kabalistic literature refers to Adam Kadmon as Tzachtzechut - The Brilliant World.

174. In so far as all the conducts of all the worlds are relative to this world, they have bounds and limitations. Even though G-d in His omnipotence could have created boundless worlds, He did not desire this, but rather chose to set aside His infinite power within creation and create finite worlds.

175. As mentioned previously, G-d is named according to His actions, therefore when his conduct changes, His name changes accordingly. This is allegorically described as one name being withdrawn and replaced by another. Thus, when G-d acts in a limitless fashion he is called Ayn Sof - The Infinite. When it arose in His will to create limited worlds, it is allegorically considered that he withdrew His limitless conduct - Ayn Sof from that "Place" wherein those worlds were destined to be, thus giving them the possibility of existence. This is called Tzimtzum Ha'Ayn Sof Boruch Hu - The constriction of the limitless. This withdrawal of the infinite conduct, which is the ultimate goodness, resulted in a condition of severity - Din proportional to the degree of its withdrawal. However, the withdrawal was not absolute, but rather a residue - Reshimu of his previous conduct remained. G-d then drew into this residue - Reshimu a limited revelation of His goodness according to the capacity of the worlds to receive. This revelation is the attribute of Mercy and is called Kav - a "Ray" or "Thread". All the conducts came about through this Ray.

176. All the divine conducts unfolded from this Ray in the following order:

1. Adam Kadmon - The Eternal Conduct;

2. His Branches - i.e.;

A. AV - Skull & Hair

B. SAG - Ears - Hearing, Nose - Smell, Mouth - Speaking (World of Akudim - Bundles)

C. BAN - Eyes - Sight, The world of Tohu, The world of Points (Din - Judgment)

D. MAH - Radiance of the Forehead, The world of Tikkun (The Joining of the conduct of mercy - MAH with Judgment - BAN.)

3. The world of Atzilut – Partzufim
   A. Atik - Malchut of Adam

Kadmon

B. Keter - Arich Anpin
   1. The Seven Repairs of the Skull (check)
   2. The Thirteen Repairs of the Beard.

C. Chochmah – Abba (Yisroel Saba - Malchut of Abba)

D. Binah – Ima (Tevunah - Malchut of Ima)

E. Zeir Anpin - Chessed, Gevurah, Tiferet, Netzach, Hod, Yesod,
   1. Yisrael,
   2. Yaakov

F. Nukvah - Malchut –
   1. Rachel,
   2. Leah,

All of these levels are explained at length in Etz Chaim.

177. The above-mentioned levels refer to the world of Atzilut and higher. Though enumerated here in a general way they are elaborated upon extensively in Etz Chaim.

Nonetheless it must be clearly understood that all the writings of the ARI"ZAL are altogether allegorical.

178. Concerning this Rabbi Chaim Vital wrote, "This is clear that supernally there is neither body nor any attribute of corporeality, G-d forbid. All these images and forms are not actual, but are merely to enable comprehension, so that man could have some understanding of these supernal conceptual matters, which are beyond his intellectual scope. Therefore, permission was given to speak in such a manner though certainly it is not thus, as scripture emphatically states "neither did you behold any image." This principle also applies to the form of the Hebrew letters which also symbolize the supernal conducts. Certainly, no letters or vowels actually exist supernally. They are merely symbolic.

179. As the RaM"CHaL states, "This is certain, that all these matters of form and corporeality which we mention in regard to the sefirot, are not possible by any stretch of the imagination, for that would be a total denial of G-d's unity. G-d forbid, as scripture explicitly states "You did not behold any images". Accordingly, the RaM"BaM explains that the prophets recieved divine communication through allegorical vision such as the Almond branch which Jeremiah beheld, that is, when G-d Blessed Be He, desired to communicate Divine concepts to the prophets, He would do so through the prophetic vision, utilizing examples that would enable the mind of the prophet to grasp these concepts. In no way did the object of the vision actually materialize. 179b. It was merely a vehicle to convey the idea. (Nonetheless not all allegories mentioned in Kabbalah are prophetic in origin.)

180. These allegories however are not arbitrary but reflect actual parallels between the Divine Conducts of Atzilut and the created realms which result from them. To illustrate, the example of the concentric circles (Igulim) parallels the spherical nature of the heavens, signifying general providence, whereas the example of the upright sefirot (Yosher), parallels the nature of Man, signifying individual providence.
These allegories, therefore, arise from the fact that matters within Man, the Universe, or the Torah result from and thus hint at the divine conducts. The Mitzvot too, correlate with

conducts, and as such may be understood through these allegories. Thus it is evident that the allegories were Divinely inspired along with their inner underlying meanings. However, caution must be taken when studying Etz Chaim, since as in all the writings of the ARI"ZAL, only the Allegory is converged without any explanation of the underlying meaning, as stated in Nefesh HaChaim, "As is known, all the words of the ARI"ZAL concerning the esoteric wisdom, are allegory".

181. The RaM"CHaL in Choker U'Mekubal suggests that when studying Kabbalah, one should first learn the Allegory alone and only later attempt to fathom its meaning. In Klach Pitchei Chochmah He refers to the allegory as "The prophetic vision", and to the meaning as "The interpretation", since both were received by Divine inspiration. The "interpretation" is found in short in his book Choker Umekubal and in some parts of Klach Pitchei Chochmah. Nonetheless it is incumbent on the reader to discern between those parts that are the "vision" and those that are the "interpretation". If one wishes to learn the allegory directly from Etz Chaim, it is advisable that he first learn only those sections entitled Mahadura Tinyana (Second Edition) and skip all else to the book. 181b. after which he may return and repeat the book in its entirety. Now, Kabbalistic writings pertaining to the three lower worlds, Briyah, Yetzirah and Asiyah, may not be entirely allegorical, for since they are created realms, actual conditions may be ascribed to them.

Chapter 9

Within which is explained the Worlds of Briyah - Creation, Yetzirah - Formation and Asiyah - Action; Palaces and Souls.

182. To this point we have discussed G-d's conducts, the ways in which He desires to act, as well as His will, providence and names, all of which are discernible through His actions. All the above constitutes the World of Atzilut - Emanation. It is called "World" merely to bring it closer to human grasp. Henceforth we will discuss the created realms.

183. The created realms are the worlds of Briyah - Creation, Yetzirah - Formation, and Asiyah - Action. When Atzilut is enumerated they constitute the four general worlds of Atzilut, Briyah, Yetzirah, and Asiyah.

184. Briyah is the Highest of the created realms and is divided into seven Palaces - Heichalot as follows:
    A. The Holy of Holies - Kodshei Kodoshim,
    B. Will - Ratzon,
    C. Love - Ahavah,

D. Merit - Zechut,
E. Brilliance - Nogah,
F. The Midst of the Heavens - Etzem HaShamayim, and
G. The Sapphire Stone - Levenat HaSapir.

These palaces are the abode of the entities which are called spirits - Roochin, Lights – Nehorin and the Holy Chayot - Chayot HaKodesh, each with its specific function all this is expounded upon at length in the Zohar and Pardes Rimonim.

185. The components of the created worlds correspond to and function as conduits for the Divine conducts of Atzilut. As explained in Zohar the seven palaces of the world of Briyah correspond to the ten sefirot as follows:

186. The first palace in ascending order is The Sapphire Stone - Levenat HaSapir. It corresponds to the sefirot of Yesod & Malchut. In this palace are angels who scrutinize ascending souls and prayers, whether to admit or reject them and who note the special merit of those who study Torah after midnight etc. This is the palace of Yosef HaTzaddik.

187. The second palace is called The Midst of the Heavens - Etzem HaShamayim. It corresponds to the sefirah of Hod. In this palace are angels who comfort the souls of those who died by the hands of the court - Beit Din, since their sins were atoned for through their death, and who engrave the memory of those who died at the hands of the Nations, to avenge their blood. Also, they scrutinize the deeds of the righteous to a hair's breadth. Furthermore, they facilitate the generous reward of those who pursue wisdom and the punishment of those who rebel against their teachers or exploit the sages, etc. This is the palace of the prophets - Heichal HaNevi'im.

188. The third palace is called Brilliance - Nogah. It corresponds to the sefirah of Netzach. In this palace are angels who oversee war & healing. On the Day of Atonement they facilitate the judgment of all matters with the exception of "Life" (which is judged in the palace of Merit - Zechut) and seal all judgments after the minchah service. Furthermore, they may also impose a spiritual ban on those deserving it. In addition they implement good reward to those who rise early to attend the morning services and who pray with a proper intent, as well as all matters pertaining to walking, such as running to perform a mitzvah, visiting the sick and drawing them toward G-d and Bringing ones children to Cheder, etc. The second & third palaces are called the palaces of the prophets.

189. The fourth palace is called Merit - Zechut. It corresponds to the sefirot of Gevurah and is the residence of the supernal court which judges the world - Beit Din Shel Ma'al. (It is called Merit - Zechut since in Judgment one's merits should be considered before his faults.) In this palace are angels who bless those who sanctify the Shabbos and curse those who desecrate it, G-d forbid. In addition, testimony is given by the angels here concerning Mans deeds. This is the palace of Yitzchak.

190. The fifth palace is called the Palace of Love - Ahavah corresponding to the conduct of Chessed. In this palace are angels who teach merit concerning Israel, and initiate love between Israel & G-d. These angels guard those who serve G-d with love and who perform acts of loving kindness. They are guardians of the secrets of the Torah. This palace houses souls before they enter the world, and is called The Palace of Avraham.

191. The sixth palace is the palace of Will corresponding to the conduct of Tiferet. In this palace are the four archangels; Michael to the right, south, corresponding to Chessed. Gavriel to the left, north, corresponding to Judgment. Refael, forward, east, and is an intermediate conduct between Chessed & Din. Uriel backward, west, and is sometimes called Nuriel. This too is an intermediate conduct, therefore when it inclines toward Chessed it is called Uriel, but when it inclines toward Din it is called Nuriel. The Acronym for these angels is A.R.Ga.Ma.N. (purple).

192. Each one of these four angels has two additional angels under him totaling twelve, three on each side, corresponding to the encampment of the 12 tribes in the desert. There are many units of 12 that correspond to these angels, some of which are: The twelve simple letters, The twelve constellations, The twelve months of the year, The twelve hours of the Day etc.

193. These four angels are the four faced angels of Ezekiels Vision as follows: Forward

Face of Man Rephael (Uriel) Intermediate Conduct East Left Face of Ox Gavriel Gevurah North Right Face of Lion Michael Chessed South Backward Face of Eagle Uriel (Rephael) Intermediate Conduct West 193b. This palace contains six additional palaces each of which has its specific angels. This is the Palace of Yaakov.

194. The seventh palace is called the Holy of Holies - Kodesh Kodoshim. This palace corresponds to the conducts of Keter, Chochmah and Binah. This level is extremely hidden and is beyond the grasp of the lower realms. Here the righteous souls of Gan Eden find delight and pleasure in G-d. Since the beings of this palace are closer to G-d than any other creatures, it is called The Throne of Glory - Kisseh HaKavod. The above mentioned six palaces of the palace of Will are called the six steps of the throne. In general, the world of Briyah is called the world of the throne.

195. The Tabernacle - Mishkan corresponded to the palaces of Will & Holy of Holies. Within the Tabernacle were ten articles which corresponded to the ten sefirot as follows; The Cherubs, the Ark-cover and the Ark corresponded to Keter, Chochmah and Binah and to the palace of the Holy of Holies. On the south was the Candleabra – Menorah corresponding to Chessed. On the north was the Table - Shulchan corresponding to Gevurah. In the middle was the Golden Alter - Mizbeach Hazahav corresponding to Tiferet. The Washstand and its Base corresponding to Netzach & Hod. The Sacrafisial Alter - Mizbeach HaOlah corresponding to Yesod and the Court - Chatzer and the Hangings - Kla'im corresponding to Malchut.

196. All the above mentioned concerns the world of Briyah. The next world, in descending order is the world of Yetzirah - Formation. This world is comprised of seven abodes. Within the highest of these, souls reside. The remaining six are the abode of the angels. These angels act as messengers in our world. Similar to the world of Briyah, these abodes correspond to the sefirot, as such the conduct of these angelic agents is determined by the abode from which they originate.

197. The world of Yetzirah is called the world of Angels. The chief angel of this world is Metatron - The Prince of the Face (Sar

HaPanim). Under him are ten categories of angels as follows:

    1. Chayot.
    2. Ophanim.
    3. Seraphim.
    4. Cherubim.
    5. Arelim.
    6. Tarshishim.
    7. Chashmalim.
    8. Elim.
    9. Malachim.
    10. Ishim As in the.
world of Briyah.

The Chayot HaKodesh, the four faced angels of Ezekiel's vision also exist here, since Ezekiel's vision was perceived on the level of Yetzirah.

198. The fourth world is called the world of Asiyah. In this world the angels are of a lesser order than in the previous worlds. The chief angel of Asiyah is Sandalfon. Within this world are 7 firmaments - Raki'im that are mentioned in the Zohar and Talmud as follows:

    1. Aravot.
    2. Ma'on.
    3. Machon.

4. Zevul.
5. Shechakim.
6. Rekiah.
7. Veelon The Ophanim.

Wheels that are mentioned in Ezekiel exist on this level. Furthermore, our physical world and all that exists within it is included as the final level of Asiyah.

199. The overseers, angels and firmaments of the world of Asiyah correspond to the ten sefirot as follows: Aravot corresponds to Keter, Chochmah & Binah Ma'on corresponds to Chessed Machon to Gevurah Zevul to Tiferet Shechakim to Netzach & Hod Rekiah to Yesod Veelon to Malchut. Earth is included as the final level of Malchut.

200. Rekiah (Yesod) of Asiyah has ten subdivisions which correspond to the sun, moon, constellations and planets.

201. The worlds of Briyah, Yetzirah and Asiyah are actual creations and their components are considered sefirot only in the sense that they correspond to the ten sefirot of Atzilut. They are therefore allegorically referred to as the Ten Sefirot of Briyah, the Ten Sefirot of Yetzirah etc.

202. G-d relates to His worlds through His Ten Divine conducts. These conducts are not manifested equally since each world receives according to its specific qualities and capacity. The apparent differences, therefore, are a result of the receiving levels rather than any change within the Giver, G-d forbid. The conducts as they relate to each specific level are termed accordingly, such as the Ten Sefirot of Briyah, the Ten Sefirot of Yetzirah etc. However, there are actually only ten general conducts and any subdivisions are merely levels within them. For example, Chessed of Briyah, Chessed of Yetzirah etc. are only levels within the general conduct of Chessed.

Since both the Divine conducts as they relate to each world and the components of the created worlds are termed Sefirot, it is incumbent upon the reader, when studying Kabbalist Literature, to discern between them.

203. As stated above, G-d is called according to His actions. As such, the Divine conducts as they are manifest within each world have specific Divine names. The Angels too are named accordingly as stated in scripture, "For my name is within Him".

204. Generally, the world of Briyah is influenced by the conduct of Binah, corresponding to Ima and the first Hey of the Divine Name (Y--H--V--H). The world of Yetzirah is primarily influenced by the conduct of the six sefirot (Chessed, Gevurah, Tiferet, Netzach, Hod, Yesod) corresponding to Zeir Anpin and the Vav of the Divine name. The world of Asiyah is primarily influenced by the conduct of Malchut, corresponding to Nukvah and the last Hey of the Name.

205. The world of Atzilut, likewise corresponds to Abba and the Yud of the Divine name, so that the four worlds together constitute the Divine name and its corresponding Parzufim - Statures as follows: Abba Ima Zeir Anpin Nukvah Atzilut Briyah Yetzirah Asiyah Yud Hey Vav Hey

206. Actually, all the influence from Atzilut comes to the created worlds through Malchut, its lowest sefirah. Therefore the above mentioned statement that the world of Briyah is influenced by Binah, refers to Binah of Malchut of Atzilut rather than the general Binah of Atzilut. The same principle applies to Yetzirah and Asiyah which are influenced by Zeir Anpin of Malchut of Atzilut and Malchut of Malchut of Atzilut. Accordingly, all the created realms are considered to be within the domain of Malchut. 206b. Everything that exists in the World of Briyah has its corresponding conduct in Atzilut. Because the concept of twelve exists in Malchut of Atzilut, it also manifests as twelve components within Briyah.

207. As stated previously, the World of Briyah was created with all its components corresponding to the Divine conducts. As such, Kabbalistic literature allegorically states that the world of Briyah "evolved" from the world of Atzilut, in that it follows the pattern of Atzilut. For example, since it was G-d's will to include His kindness in the conduct of the World, He created the Palace of Love - Heichal Ha'Ahava in Briyah, and since it was also His will to include Judgement - Din, He created the Palace of Merit - Heichal Zechut, within which the world is judged. This principle applies to all the components of Briyah. 207b. Thus it can be said that the palace of Love "evolved" from the sefirah of Chessed, and the palace of Merit, from that of Gevurah etc. However, obviously there is no developmental progression of "evolution" between Atzilut and the created realms whatsoever, but rather, all creation was brought in to being ex nihilo. Any other consideration would be erroneous.

208. The Human Soul consists of five (5) levels corresponding to the five Partzufim and the letters of G-d's name as follows: The thorn of the Yod Yud First Hey Vav Last Hey Adam Kadmon Atzilut Briyah Yetzirah Asiyah Yechidah Chayah Neshamah Ruach Nefesh the GR"A wrote that the levels of the Nefesh and Ruach are predominant in Man, especially Ruach which is his essential identity. It is the Ruach that receives reward and punishment, is cognigant, possesses faculties and is conscious of the senses. Upon its departure death results. The Neshamah is a higher level which is generally beyond our consciousness. It is the source of Divine guidance and inspiration. In this sense it is sometimes referred to as a person's Mazal or Malach since it influences him from above. Occasionally one may experience an inspirational flash from the Neshamah level which guides him and elevates his awareness. Therefore, the term Ruach refers to Mans essential identity, whereas Neshamah refers to that which guides him from above. 8 For this reason the term Neshamah may often include within it, both Chaya and Yechidah.

209. The world of Briyah is on the highest spiritual level of the created realms and is the closest to G-dliness (i.e. Atzilut). It receives Divine influence directly from Atzilut without any intermediary level. In Briyah the spiritual entities themselves may be either of the aspects of Ruach or Nefesh. Those of Ruach are called Ruchin (spirits) and those of Nefesh are called Nehorin (lights). Since the aspect of Neshamah comes to Briyah directly from Atzilut their Neshamah is considered to be actual G-dliness.

210. The beings in the world of Yetzirah receive their Neshamah through Briyah. As a result, they receive only a minute portion from Atzilut itself. This portion is called Chayah - Living.

211. The beings in the world of Asiyah receive their Neshamah through Yetzirah. Only those individuals who have special merit may receive a minute influence from Briyah. This influence is called "Chayah". Those who are even more meritorious may further receive an influence from Atzilut.

This influence is called Yechidah (Unique). To summarize: the level of G-dliness in Asiyah is called Yechidah that of Yetzirah is called Chayah, and that of Briyah is called Neshamah, all of which is explained by the GR"A in Sifra D'Tzniuta.

212. The GR"A states in his comments on Zohar - Heichalot that in all worlds the G-dly aspect (which is received from above, similar to prophetic inspiration) is called Neshamah. This in no way contradicts his above statement. In Sifra D'Tzniuta he deals with each world specifically, as it relates to other worlds, whereas here he is referring to all the created worlds collectively as they relate to Atzilut. Only that which comes from Atzilut (i.e. Chaya of Yetzirah & Yechidah of Asiyah) is truly considered Neshamah. All other levels of the created worlds (i.e. Neshamah of Yetzirah & Chayah of Asiyah etc.) come from Ruach and Nefesh of Briyah and thus cannot be regarded as Neshamah.

213. The GR"A wrote, "You should know with certainty that Moshe Rabbeinu, perceived only on the level of Briyah in the palace of Will, as stated by Rabbi Moshe Cordovero and the Ari"Zal. The remaining prophets perceived on the level of Yetzirah. Daniel perceived the pinnacle of Asiyah which is the floor of Yetzirah, since he was an intermediate level between the prophets & subsequent generations. Since then, with each generation perception has diminished, until in these latter generations we perceive only on the level of the "heels" of Asiah. 213b. Since each world contains within itself aspects of all other worlds, it is possible through allegory to comprehend on our level matters concerning Adam Kadmon, Atzilut, Briyah, Yetzirah and Asiyah, though we have no direct perception of them. Even the prophet Ezekiel who received his prophecy outside of the Land of Israel during the end of the first Temple, spoke in riddles, the depth of which we cannot fathom, so too the prophecy of Zechariah was in the form of sealed visions. We will not fully understand the meaning of their words until we are divinely enlightened (in the Messianic era).

Chapter 10

Within which the matter of Sitra Achera and the complete repair in the time to come are explained.

214. Now, just as G-d, blessed be He, created the worlds of Briyah, Yetzirah and Asiyah as instruments to affect goodness and holiness, so too He created entities which are instrumental in affecting the evil which He deems necessary in the world. [This is in order to bring about the conditions of free choice.] These forces are generally termed Sitra Achera, that is, the "Other Side", the side of evil, G-d forbid. Even though G-d's will is good, He created evil as a temporary existence in order to bring about the ultimate good. The very existence of evil therefore is solely to realize this goodness, as stated, "Everything that G-d does is for His sake".

215. The agents of Sitra Achara have three functions. The first is to seduce man to sin through which he becomes impure, as stated in Gemara (Yoma), "When man acts impurely below, He is made impure from above." These forces from which the Yetzer Hara -

Evil inclination stems, draw man toward sin by causing it to appear sweet and pleasant, as stated, "Sweet is stolen water". The Zohar refers to this as "The pleasure with impurities". None the less the purpose in their creation is to merit the righteous. Through conquering the evil inclination, which seems? insurmountable, the righteous are rewarded in direct proportion to their effort, as stated, "According to the difficulty is the reward". All this is explained at length in the Zohar through the allegory of the king who sent a harlot to seduce his son. He stipulated to her that if she succeeds all the goodness that would have rightly been given to his son would be hers instead. But, if he shunned her advances the prince would receive great reward and she too would be rewarded since through her great efforts he merited this goodness. Throughout, the fathers' intent was for the good of his son, and even the Harlot, though she appeared in the guise of a temptress, was the king's agent and secretly desired the prince's success.

216. The second function of the Sitra Achara is to accuse and summons a soul to judgment, G-d forbid, as stated in the Zohar, "G-d made it, that they fear Him - that He created an accuser who demands judgment, and that the concept of punishment exists, so that there will be a fear of G-d in the world.

217. The third function is to mete out punishment upon the sinners, either in this world or in Gehenom. All this is to fulfill G-d's desire to conduct the world through justice as stated, "for all His ways are just". All the above fall into the category of Sitra Achara and are called Kelipot - Husks. Holiness - Kedusha is called Pri - Fruit and they are as husks surrounding the fruit.

218. There are four general Kelipot which are alluded to in Ezekiels vision, as written, "And I saw and behold a storm wind coming from the north, a great cloud, and a roaring fire encompassed by a glow". They are also alluded to in Eliyahu's vision, Ruach - Wind, Ra'ash - Earthquake, Esh - Fire, within which G-d was not revealed plus a Kol Dmama Daka - a still small voice.

219. Of these four, three are completely evil. The fourth, which is Kelipat Nogah - the glowing husk, may be transformed to goodness. The Brit Milah - Circumcision consists of three steps corresponding to the three impure Kelipot. They are the removal of the foreskin - Arlah, the pulling back of the remaining skin - Priah, and the letting of a drop of blood - Tipat Dam. In addition the verse in Genesis refering to Tohu - formless, Vohu - emptiness, Choshech - darkness, and Ruach Elokim - the spirit of G-d, corresponds to these four Kelipot.

220. G-d created everything with its counterpart. Therefore, just as He created the three holy levels of Briyah, Yetzirah and Asiyah, so too He created the Briyah, Yetzirah and Asiyah of Kelipah as their counterparts.

221. In respect to the "created" realms of holiness only three levels exist. However they have the benefit of G-ds influence and revelation which rests upon them from His Divine conducts, i.e. Atzilut. The Sitra Achara on the other hand does not receive such influence from above. 221b. Rather, an additional world of Sitra Achara called Atzilut of Kelipah was created as a counterpart to Atzilut of Kedusha, so that Sitra Achara & Kedusha would have the same number of corresponding parts. However, unlike Atzilut of Kedusha, which represents

G-d's Divine conducts, Atzilut of Kelipah is merely a created world and as such they are not comparable.

222. Though the order of the levels of Kelipah correspond to those of Kedusha, Atzilut of Kelipah being itself created does not stand above the created realms of Kedush. Rather it is opposite the Holy of Holies of the world of Briyah, since no created thing can rise higher than that level.

223. Furthermore, the seven palaces of Briyah of Kedusha have their counterparts in Sitra Achara. They are called "the seven impure palaces". Their names in rising order are: Bor - the pit Shachat - death Duma - silence Chova - debt Sheol - the grave Tzalmavet - the shadow of death Eretz Tachteet - the netherworld 223b. These in turn correspond to the seven names of the Yetzer Hara as follows: Rah - The evil one Tameh - The impure one Soneh - The enemy Even Michshol - The stumbling block Arel - The uncircumcised one Satan - Satan Tzafoni - The northerner The Zohar explains at length the specific purpose of each of these. Generally, the agents of Kelipah have the opposite function to those of Kedusha. In addition, Sitra Achara also consists of ten sefirot which are called "the ten sefirot of Kelipah" or "the substitute palaces".

224. Because G-d desired to conduct the world with judgment as well as kindness, He created the Sitra Achara. As such, the Sitra Achara is considered to have come out of the attribute of judgment since that is its sole purpose, without which it would not have been created.

225. As stated above, initially G-d manifested the attribute of total judgment, represented by the name of 52 - Ban. He then joined to it the attribute of mercy represented by the name of 45 - Mah, in order to bring about its rectification. Since Sitra Achara comes about solely from the judgment of Ban - 52, the gradual rectification brought about through Mah - 45 diminishes its function so that ultimately with the final rectification, Sitra Achara will cease to exist. Part will be transformed into holiness and the remainder will be obliterated.

226. The existence of the Yetzer Hara and the Sitra Achara is only necessary during the six millennia of this world which follow the conduct of the six sefirot - Chessed, Gevurah, Tiferet, Netzach, Hod & Yesod as stated in Talmud, "You have given us the Yetzer Hara for the sole purpose of earning merit." However, beginning with the seventh millennium which is the world to come and is a time of reward, (and certainly after the tenth millennium, which is the eternal conduct of Adam Kadmon) its purpose will be abrogated & the Talmud states, "In the future the Holy One Blessed Be He shall slaughter (abrogate) the Yetzer Hara".

This is further supported by the scriptural verses, "I will withdraw the impure spirit from the earth" and, "I shall remove the heart of stone from your flesh". In addition, concerning the world to come scripture states, "And I shall give you a heart of flesh and I shall instill a new spirit in your midst and cause you to walk in my statutes", and, "Hashem shall be King upon the entire earth, on that day, Hashem shall be one and His name one." Even in this world the Sitra Achara may be abrogated on a specific spiritual level by the complete rectification of that level. It then only exists on a lesser level. But concerning the world to come it is stated, "Death shall be swallowed forever", and the world will be perfected in G-d's Kingdom. This will constitute complete rectification in which "G-d will be one and His name one".

May it be G-d's will that we merit this speedily in our days through Kindness and Mercy - Amen.

www.ingramcontent.com/pod-product-compliance
Lightning Source LLC
Chambersburg PA
CBHW070149080526
44586CB00015B/1912